Prais

"When it comes to voc........, ... is all in. There aren't many books on the subject that you might call passionate, even courageous, *and* practical. This is one of them. I am well past the beginning stage of a career, but I found his discussion of the difference between vocation and identity to be helpful. You can still be you, even if your future is unclear. For anyone who is on the way—and that's many of us—this book will be a wonderful source of guidance."
—Richard Lischer, author of *Just Tell the Truth: A Call to Faith, Hope, and Courage*

"Drew Tucker is one of those voices moving the collective thought of progressive Christianity forward. It's not often these days that straight, white, Christian men have a sincere grassroots impact on their diverse communities, but Tucker makes the leap and is attentive to his role in lifting and launching others. Between his contribution to *The Deconstructionists Playbook* and his work sculpting young minds at the university level, he has proven himself in *4D Formation* to be a thought leader and guiding light."
—Crystal Cheatham (she/her), Black queer Christian; creator of Our Bible App; host of the podcast *Lord Have Mercy*; and coeditor of *The Deconstructionists Playbook: An Anthology*

"Not since Parker Palmer's *Let Your Life Speak* have I read such a helpful and compelling guide for discerning life's callings. Part practical, part personal, part pastoral, and entirely profound, *4D Formation* accompanies readers in their journey through discovery, discernment, development, and decision-making. I especially appreciate Drew Tucker's full inclusion of multiple religious and secular voices, even as he plumbs the depths of his own Christian worldview. This book will help you live life well, and the world will flourish as a result."

—Jason A. Mahn, author of *Neighbor Love through Fearful Days: Finding Purpose and Meaning in a Time of Crisis*

"Tucker gives us a clear challenge and opportunity to discover, engage, and connect with our very reason for being."

—Lamont Anthony Wells, director, LuMin Network/ ELCA Campus Ministry, and president, African Descent Lutheran Association (ELCA)

"How many times in life have you been stymied, uncertain about what to do next? It happens to all of us, from children to people well into their retirement years. While Tucker writes from the perspective of a teacher, pastor, and mentor of college students, he knows that discerning how to spend our days in meaningful and life-giving ways is a seasonal, if not a daily decision. His writing is rich, artistic, and clear—and his thoughts are drawn from the deep wells of religion, philosophy, psychology, science, and race and gender studies. Filled with pertinent anecdotes and wisdom gained from hearing and dealing with intense questions about vocation and identity, *4D Formation* offers indispensable guidance for those who are seeking to determine their next step."

—Clay Schmit, professor of preaching, Emmanuel Academies, Naples, Florida

4D Formation

4D
FORMATION

Exploring Vocation
in Community

Drew Tucker

Fortress Press
Minneapolis

4D FORMATION
Exploring Vocation in Community

Cover design: Kristin Miller

Print ISBN: 978-1-5064-7398-7
eBook ISBN: 978-1-5064-7399-4

*To all the students, past and present, who invited me
to be a part of their vocational exploration*

Contents

Preface

For more than a decade, I've worked first as a lay minister and then a pastor on college campuses, accompanying students who aren't just earning degrees but exploring their purpose. On one hand, these schools are very different contexts. The student profiles at large state universities like the University of South Carolina are quite different from those of two-year institutions like New River Community College. The global recognition of Virginia Tech is a stark contrast to the regional familiarity of Radford University. The endowments of Duke University are, shall we say, quite a bit larger than those of small private schools like Capital University.

Yet in each place, I've found students on a common journey: exploring their vocations, without certainty about what the word *vocation* means in the first place. Not only did students need to understand vocation as a concept, but even more, they needed practices to help them clarify what vocations they would choose to live. So over these eleven years, I've developed a model of vocational exploration that can help not just college students but anyone who is wondering what their purpose is and how it fits into the grand scheme of things.

Though the content you'll read was developed throughout my career, the book was truly born in the Covid-19 pandemic. In the early stages, as I worked from home and reflected on the work of college ministry prior to the pandemic, I realized I was at a transition point in my career. Not only had my job become more administrative, but I'd also begun a doctoral program. If I was ever going to publish a book on this topic, it was the right time in history. My work-from-home arrangements meant I could more manageably write a book while working full time. Because this is my first book, the entire publishing process has been an opportunity for me to practice what I preach: discovering options, discerning priorities, developing skills, and deciding what next steps to take. The result is now in your hands (or on your screen). I hope you like the book, but more than that, I hope it is useful for you.

Acknowledgments

While authors often get sole credit for the creation of a book, a whole village comes together to bring them to birth. This book emerged from a number of communities that inspired its evolution. In trying to thank everyone, I'll surely miss important contributors, so I apologize for those omissions. Still, I think it is important to try to name those whose influence gave life to this project.

Without Beth Gaede and the team at Fortress Press taking a chance on a new author, this enterprise would have been impossible. Thank you for trusting me!

Thanks also to the generous support of Trinity Lutheran Church (Ashland, OH), St. Peter Evangelical Lutheran Church (Norwalk, OH), and Augsburg Lutheran Church (Orrville, OH), who provided financial support during the writing and editing process.

I'm indebted to the support of students, faculty, staff, and supporters of Capital University and Trinity Lutheran Seminary, the community in which much of this 4D Formation model is incarnate. To them, and to all my students and colleagues from Duke University (and Duke Lutherans), the University of South Carolina (and Gamecock Lutherans), Radford University (and Highlander Lutherans), New River Community College, Lenoir-Rhyne University, and Virginia Tech (and The Well), thank you for giving me the chance to minister alongside, teach with, and learn from you.

To Rick Lischer, thank you for taking interest in me when I felt like I was out of my depth, for good breakfasts, and for conversations that still energize me a decade later. I'm forever grateful for your support.

Some classmates become colleagues, and colleagues become friends, and friends become family. Thanks to Bobby and Amanda Rackley, the Clergy Crash Crew of Lutheran Theological Southern Seminary, Dikiea Elery, Adam Baker, Rayner Jae Liu, and so many others who have inspired me to be a better leader, a better pastor, a better writer, a better student, and just plain better.

A number of mentors have formed me as a leader. To Clay Schmit, thank you for making space in your administrative schedule to mentor me and remind me that theology is, in part, an art. To Christie Lohr Sapp and Jacqueline Bussie, thank you for teaching me meaningful modes of interfaith leadership. To John Wertz, thank you for bearing with my naivete without suffocating my idealism. To Crystal Cheatham, Dr. Jason Mahn, and Rev. Lamont Anthony Wells: thank you for taking the time to read advance copies and to offer your glowing recommendations. You are incredible partners in ministry. And while I'm thankful for all those who've pastored me over the years, Walt Jordan first saw in me a call to ministry long before I thought of it for myself. As he rests now with the saints, his memory is still a blessing.

I come from a family of voracious readers, writers, thinkers, singers, and talkers (a few of you talk more than most). To the Tuckers, Albrights, Edds, McCrorys, Contis, Browns, and Wayts: thank you for teaching me the value of words—written, spoken, thought, and sung.

A special thanks to my parents: my mom for instilling in me the love of reading and my dad for believing in me far more than I believe in myself. Though their deaths are long past, my grandparents Dale and Doris Albright and Frank and Jeanette Tucker established a legacy for our family to which I'm forever indebted.

Karen Wayt, Kim Conti, Cameron Bowersock, Noah Fischbach, and Samantha DiBiaso read early drafts, offered excellent feedback, and shaped the final form, for which I'm eternally grateful.

To my wife, Michelle, who's edited most everything I've written and always made it better: I'm sorry for all the comma splices and incomplete thoughts. If any typos were missed, it certainly wasn't your fault. I love you.

My faith has changed so much in my life, as has my understanding of God. That should become evident in the pages that follow in ways that may challenge you or that bring you comfort. In the midst of all that spiritual evolution, I have not forgotten my gratitude to God. I'm thankful that the author of the universe remained with me as I wrote this book. I'm grateful that as my beliefs change, God remains ever present. Without that inspiration and that presence, this book would never have been born.

I hope that whatever else might come of your reading of this, something in it points you toward a sacred mystery of love and life that permeates all the cosmos.

Introduction

Here's my first challenge: don't put this book down the first time you come across a weird word or strange concept. I promise to do my best to define those words and detail those concepts because you're worth it, and your vocation is worth it.

And there it is, one of those strange groupings of apparently alien syllables: vocation.

This concept is most often used in two places, at least in my experience: churches and universities. Yet that word— *vocation*—is frequently deployed as insider language, which means it's rarely defined and therefore often misunderstood by insiders and outsiders alike. And I know this especially because I'm a pastor who works in a university! So many people use the word *vocation* in my circles, and too often, they use it to mean different things, sometimes even conflicting things.

So let me offer a clear definition now to guide the rest of the book's reflections. Vocation is *any meaningful, life-giving work for the world.* I'll remind you of that over and again. You'll probably get tired of me saying it. I apologize in advance, but it's so important to have a shared understanding that I'm willing to take the risk. Plus, as my wife and students will tell you, I don't mind being annoying from time to time in order to emphasize a point worth making.

You'll encounter other challenges to this study that we mustn't ignore. First off, there's the "religious stuff." Odds are, you don't share my religious tradition, the Lutheran branch of Christianity, particularly the shoot known as the Evangelical Lutheran Church in America (ELCA). In fact, the odds are growing that you either identify with a religion other than Christianity or don't identify with any religious group at all.

That's OK. This book is still for you.

You see, part of my job at Capital University, a school affiliated with the ELCA, is to provide support for the spiritual wellness of all our students, faculty, and staff across our religious traditions. This work brings Lutherans and Buddhists, atheists and Muslims, Jains and Wiccans, agnostics and Hindus, and spiritual but not religious people together to talk about our life's meaning, purpose, and work. We all come together to talk about vocation, even if we don't always use the same language. This focus on vocation, influenced by a host of different religions and worldviews, connects with my work over the past ten years as a campus minister and professor at community colleges, private institutions, and public universities. I'm passionate about empowering those I work with to find ways of being in the world that are life-giving for others and meaningful to themselves across religious, racial, ethnic, gender, and sexual identities.

So while I use God language, since it's the spiritual language authentic to my tradition, I encourage you to insert your own understanding of holiness, or spirituality, or the divine, or transcendent. I believe that vocation, widely understood as a concept within the Christian tradition, is accessible and appropriate for people of all faith backgrounds. Or at least, it should be. That's my intent with this book: to empower readers across various faith traditions with concepts and tools to explore their vocations. In fact, you'll notice as you read along that I've gleaned vocational wisdom from many religious and spiritual traditions. It's important to consider this broader set of perspectives as we explore vocation together.

Another, quite different problem is this: many people don't feel like they have time to worry about vocation, and others can't afford to focus on anything that's not immediately practical to their survival. When you're living paycheck to paycheck, ruminating on life's purpose seems trivial. When you're wealthy enough to live on the beach, summer in the mountains, and vacation across the globe, then vocation seems rather uninteresting. For those of us in the middle, not at all rich and yet comfortably middle class, our schedules are packed with classes, work, sports and music lessons for the kids, yoga and the gym for the parents, and house chores enough for all. Combine this with the entertainment of screens in every room, in our pockets, and in our bags, and it seems there's just no time to figure out what work might be meaningful and life-giving, no matter how nice it might be for life to have a deeper meaning.

I'm here to tell you that life already has a deeper meaning, and comprehending your callings will invigorate your career and your hobbies, your family and your citizenship. Vocation is more than another voice competing with the other distractions of life. Vocation is the bedrock that supports your life in the midst of all the distractions. Vocation is the call that cuts through the noise, the lighthouse that draws you to shore through dangerous waters, the melody that turns cacophony into harmony. For every one of us, no matter our social strata, our lives have purpose. Clarity around your vocations helps you comprehend that purpose in ways that shape your decisions, your calendar, your spending, your relationships, your entire life.

And there's a different problem altogether: I said *vocations*. Plural. None of us—no one—has only one vocation.

There are lots of ways you make meaning with your life and many different methods for meeting other peoples' needs. Sometimes choosing a vocational path means giving up other opportunities, but not always. In fact, I claim over a dozen vocations right now! While I will talk about vocation broadly as a concept, I will also address ways that our different vocations relate to one another. Later chapters describe how these vocations relate to, shape, and support one another.

Within all these complications, there's something wonderfully, powerfully true. Your identity and your work have both present meaning and lasting purpose. While there's certainly a layer of mystery, there are also practical steps you can take to both discover and develop your vocations. This is why I, along with others, refer to the process as vocational *exploration*. Like an explorer in new lands, you're facing a landscape that demands your attention and has within it the resources for abundant life. Like our universe, some of it will remain a holy mystery even as we explore farther and farther into the stars.

The last reason I don't want you to put this down when you're challenged? Because, at its core, this book is meant to challenge you. I mean to challenge you in this specific way: to live a more meaningful, life-giving existence that blesses you, your community, the world beyond, even all creation.

Ultimately, the goal of this book is to equip you with a conceptual framework to understand vocation and practical tools to explore your vocation. I want you to understand what you can and can't control in this holy endeavor and to introduce you to a diversity of vocational explorers whose wisdom can help you on your journey. To begin that exploration, let's lay out a basic trajectory for our journey.

A Journey

Some people think that there's only one possible path for them, that God has only one very specific life in mind, and that any departure from that path is a sin, a deviation from God's intent. I call this the "my way or the highway" approach to vocation. In short, people assume any variation from this singular plan displeases God and devalues their lives.

Those people couldn't be more wrong.

Others treat vocation like a certain, predetermined destiny—that no matter what they do, they'll find their one vocation exactly as they're supposed to. I call this the "all roads lead to Rome" approach. These people seem to think that simply by virtue of existence, the meaning of life will reveal itself to you.

As much as I wish that were true, that we would all simply happen upon our callings organically, the plague of depression and anxiety that I see firsthand among youth and young adults trying to decipher their vocations tells me that this doesn't match most people's experience. A sense of purpose and of being valued won't cure mental illness, to be sure, but it can provide essential scaffolding for wellness.

I'm here to tell you that there's more than one path for you to walk in this life and that there's a blessing on many of those roads. Yet there is one road that certainly won't lead you to Rome: the one you never take. To find your vocations, you must explore. Just waiting won't lead you to your vocations. You have to search out options, exercise opportunities, evaluate your priorities, and choose your next path. God's not about only blessing specific paths; God's about blessing the journey itself. As I like to say to my students, the process *is* the product. This means some trails will wind wildly, others will require vertical climbs, and still others will have dead ends. None of that means you're on the wrong path, for if you're pursuing your vocation, that's a journey God blesses. Even if a particular road doesn't lead to your vocation, it will clarify your skills and your values and maybe even alert you to what is not your vocation.

A Map, a Legend, and a Compass

To state the obvious, not every journey begins with a map. Sometimes you chart a course into the unknown, à la *Star Trek*'s mission to "go where no one has gone before."

Fortunately for you, many people—billions, in fact—have lived their vocations, have explored their vocations, have changed their vocations, and have left evidence of their processes. Some of them have even left their reflections in art and literature, in history and politics. In that sense, others have left maps with their courses charted, their journeys detailed. You'll find this map not in Waze or on Google but in the stories others share of their lives, in memoirs and music, in paintings and conversations that detail the ways in which they explored their vocations.

While such resources can certainly help you, those journeys are not your journey. Others may have walked this landscape before, but geography can change. While the maps made before will help you along the way, you've got to update them. Sometimes you have to draw your own boundaries. At other times, you must cut your own trails. The changes in the landscape mean that the tactics used by others won't necessarily work for you. You've got to try things out and find what works best for you. Further, you have capacities different from others', so you might find a different route altogether because of your unique gifts. We'll talk more about maps in chapters 3 and 4.

Legends tell you how to read maps. For instance, in the bottom right of Google Maps is a line that tells you how many inches of screen relate to the actual length of geography. On Waze, as you approach an obstacle or event of interest, the legend appears on the screen to alert you to the pressing concern. Paper maps often include symbols—for instance, circles might signify regular cities, while stars could stand for state capitals. Solid red lines may stand for interstates, dotted red lines for US highways, and black lines for state and local roads. Green areas for natural preserves of some kind and white areas for private land. You get the idea. Yet without a legend, you couldn't know how to decipher the various colors, shapes, and lines.

In one sense, there's no digital or paper map for your journey of vocation, so there's no legend to help you make sense of vocational landmarks. In another sense, the most updated maps of your world—maps of roads and buildings, geography and topography, communities and nature preserves—are the maps for your vocation. Your vocation happens in the life that you lead, in the context where you live, in the settings of your life. Yet it's not just the static features—the streets and hills, rivers and buildings—that constitute a map for your growth; it's the people who drive the roads and walk the hills, who swim in the rivers and inhabit the buildings. So the legend for your map should point out the places you can explore *and* the people who join you on the journey. For us, that's 4D Formation, which we'll talk about in part 2 of the book.

When we think of a compass, most often our first thought goes to that little circle that looks kind of like a watch, but instead of telling time, it uses the earth's magnetic field to tell you which way is north. All the pieces of your map might change. Roads get closed, green hills become neighborhoods, features evolve. Even so, the directions remain constant. North is always north.

On this journey, our faith or spirituality, that transcendent connection to our source of life, acts as our compass and keeps us oriented in this changing world. You'll see me reference this in my God language. Faith points to our spiritual true north and aligns our journey as we explore our vocations. Whatever your faith is, hold fast to it. One of the reasons I use faith language throughout this book is because my own faith provides grounding, inspiration, and challenge throughout my vocational journeys. If my perspective is different from yours, that's fine. Use your own spiritual compass and the tools in this book to chart your own vocational journey.

It's important to note that God isn't the compass. Why make the distinction? Because compasses break. Compasses can be temporarily disoriented when magnets come close. Compasses are limited tools that we create. This means something subtle yet significant: our faith isn't God. Whatever faith you have, whatever gods or eternal truths or ultimate realities that ground all being—that thing is beyond even the compass itself. God is the magnetic field that makes the compass point north in the first place. You'll see hints of this compass guiding throughout the book.

A Mission

The mission of this book is simple: to empower you to explore your vocations. How am I going to do that? In the chapters that follow, I'll first describe the nature of vocation and then empower you with tools, both knowledge and practical skills, to explore your vocations.

The first part of the book introduces vocation as a concept and provides a framework for understanding how calling works in our lives.

Chapter 1, "God Calls You," starts a fight with vocation guru Frederick Buechner. Well, not a fight exactly. This chapter addresses why Buechner's oft-used definition for vocation is insufficient for robust vocational exploration in the twenty-first century. More than that, I offer an original definition, one based in multifaith dialogue and over a decade of work with young adults exploring their vocations on college campuses across the United States. This definition also points to the reason we must seek wisdom from many different kinds of people when exploring our vocations.

Chapter 2, "Defining Our Terms," talks about the differences and similarities between your vocations and identities. More importantly, I emphasize why you shouldn't build your identity solely on your vocations, because many vocations don't last forever.

Chapter 3, "You Are Called Wholly," emphasizes that you're called with your identities, experiences, and abilities, not despite them. This means that your skills and your challenges, your capacities and inabilities, your race and sexual orientation, your gender expression and legal status, your resources and your needs—they're all part of the you who is called to a vocation. God calls your whole self, so bringing your whole self to your vocations will increase your appreciation of and participation in them.

Chapter 4, "Called through Your Communities," considers the ways in which we encounter calls in our lives. Often religious, educational, or civic communities play a significant role, as do mentors who've gone on this journey before us. Our embodied experiences—the physical, mental, and spiritual history we bear—also act as conduits through which we're called to vocations. God's call is not in spite of the things that you wish were different about your family or the talents you don't have; rather, God calls you with and through the things that make your life story.

Chapter 5, "Called for Transcendent Mission," connects your callings with transcendent purpose. In fact, it's that transcendent purpose—which I know as God's mission—that grounds and directs your particular vocations. This focus on purpose beyond yourself also reminds you that even when you feel isolated by your calling, you're not alone in your vocation because you're connected with a boundless network of saints working for the reconciliation of all things. It then shifts to the specific vocations to which you may be called. These can occur simultaneously and in a number of different arenas, including family, career, society, and religious contexts. You are called to something that is meaningful for you and life-giving for the world, which can be many things. Your vocations are not just jobs, or ways to make money, or burdens of obligation. They're stations in life that fulfill holy purpose for you and for others.

The second part of the book turns to a specific model of vocational exploration that I call 4D Formation.

Chapter 6, "Discovering What's Possible," begins a new section and offers practices to explore vocational possibilities. This doesn't have to be scary or intimidating! This section introduces 4D Formation, a process through which you can clarify what you're called to and what you're not (at least not right now), beginning with discovery. To know your vocation, you must first know what options exist.

Discovery, then, is a necessary part of vocational exploration. This chapter details activities for vocational discovery,
drawing on high-impact practices popularized in higher education. This discussion both reveals that we can hold multiple vocations at the same time and considers the importance
of mentors in the journey of developing vocation who can
introduce practices and experiences along the way.

Chapter 7, "Demystifying Discernment," offers a definition of *discernment*, since that's another churchy word
that often is left undefined or used differently by different
people. In this process, to discern is to prioritize the value
of something in your life. As you explore vocational possibilities, discernment assesses how well those possibilities
fit with your identity, your skills, your limitations, and your
understanding of God's mission. Some options are exciting but don't relate to your passions or commitment. Others
don't thrill but seem significant. This chapter offers tools
for discernment, including asset mapping, priority matrixes,
and meditation, as well as invites conversation about internal and external calls.

Chapter 8, "Developing Your Skills," emphasizes that
vocations don't just randomly appear in your life. While
discovery leads you to options and discernment clarifies
value, you need to develop the skills related to your vocational priorities. Practice never makes perfect, but it sure
makes you better. Experience—through internships, community service, and gamified reality—can help hone the talents you bring, and in turn, those talents can reinforce the
value of your potential vocations.

Chapter 9, "Deciding What's Next," begins by acknowledging that our culture has a love-hate relationship with
decisions. Try to decide with your family where to eat
dinner, and a chorus of "I don't care" will arise. Yet North

American culture seems to force college decisions on teens earlier every year. We know we're capable of decisions, but we often treat those decisions as final rather than temporary. This chapter highlights a different way to make decisions that both encourages the necessity and emphasizes the temporary nature of decisions. In the words of the Forum for Theological Exploration (FTE) and ELCA Young Adults, vocational decisions are simply about your "next most faithful step." Having employed discovery, discernment, and development, now is the time to remember that God's already ahead of you, blessing any holy path you might choose. This also emphasizes that the process isn't linear. These practices don't demand a step-by-step execution; instead, they're habits to develop so that when situations arise in life that seem challenging or confusing, this set of tools is ready to deploy.

A Launch

So now it's time to launch into the journey itself. Just by selecting this book and committing to considering its contents, you're already on a path of vocational exploration. You may disagree with some of what I say; that's fine. You may find inspiration; I hope you do. But by undertaking the process itself, you're opening yourself to a deeper awareness of meaningful, life-giving work in your life, for the world. Let's get started.

Part 1

Understanding Vocation

Since vocation is a concept that's not used clearly or consistently, this first section takes a step-by-step approach to understanding not just the definition of *vocation* but the ways we experience that calling. This notion of being called in the first place evokes a number of questions: Who is calling us? How are we called? Why are we called? The chapters in this section answer those questions and offer some conceptual tools to frame our understanding as we explore our purpose.

This section also addresses the distinction between our identities and our vocations. We often confuse the two in ways that seem harmless but can lead to destructive patterns of thought. One danger is assuming that our vocations are our identities, while another is assuming that our worth is wrapped up with our performance of our vocations. Understanding our vocations clearly can also help us have a clearer conception of our identities and our worth.

As you work through this section, take notes about the things you disagree with or want to learn more about as you explore your vocation. That's part of constructing your own map on this journey of purpose. Not only can you disagree with other vocational explorers; you can disagree with me as I introduce the concepts to you. The resource list at the end of the book is a good place to find other approaches to vocation in paper and digital media, which give you other maps to consider and landmarks to add to your own chart. Also make notes of the places that inspire you or that you want to incorporate into your life more intentionally so that you can come back to them to reflect as you continue your journey.

Chapter 1

God Calls You

I'll never forget the first time I heard Frederick Buechner's famous definition of *vocation*. I was on the golf course with Pastor Dave and a few other people from the local United Methodist congregation (UMC). Though I've spent all of my conscious life as a Lutheran, the local UMC had a praise band where I could play my drums and a bigger youth group led by the girl I was dating. Like any adolescent who kind of liked Jesus and really liked attention, I started attending that church and playing in the praise band.

Like many people my age, I was also swept up in the golf craze birthed by Tiger Woods's dominance. I'd played golf before I saw Tiger play, but truthfully, it never really spiked my passion or held my attention. Watching Tiger—a man of African, Asian, and Indigenous American descent—crush the competition on courses where his ancestors would have been barred from play, I was inspired not just to play the game he played but to find a passion and purpose for my life, much in the way he'd found one in professional golf.

So there we were, on a long par five, crossing the creek to reach our drives, when Pastor Dave asked me what I wanted to do with my life. At this point, I honestly can't remember the flavor of the day. Seminary was always an option, but so were a host of other possibilities: teaching in public schools, pursuing a career as a professional musician, and for two nanoseconds—very brief, very different, very wrong nanoseconds, I might add—joining the military or attending law school. While I don't recall whatever it was that I told Pastor Dave at that moment, he responded with Buechner's oft-quoted line, one that was seared into my memory: "The place God calls you to is the place where your deep gladness and the world's deep hunger meet."[1]

How great is that? My vocation, my life's greatest purpose, is where I'm glad meeting other people's needs. Given the fact that I heard this on the golf course, where I very often feel glad—except when I knock a brand-new Pro V1x golf ball into a lake or the woods, of course—it's no surprise this description of vocation was alluring. God wants me happy, I thought. I deserve to be glad! I'll know my vocation, my holy purpose, whenever I'm happy.

I couldn't have been more wrong.

Depending on your dictionary of preference, the definitions of *gladness* vary slightly. Yet in every case I've found, the first definition always includes the feeling or experience of happiness, joy, pleasure, or contentment. In other words, to most people who speak English, *gladness* is roughly equivalent to "feeling happy." As a teenager, that's what I understood Buechner to mean, so that's the experience of vocation I sought for much of my young adulthood. That's also the definition of gladness I encounter most often on college campuses.

That journey, pursuing gladness as a necessary benchmark of my vocation, nearly led me off the rails. As I said earlier, I genuinely like attention, so of course I feel a sense of gladness when I'm noticed. Sometimes, that meant I felt false fulfillment when I was noticed for unhealthy things. Perhaps the best example here comes from one of the worst experiences of my life: my years-long bout with an eating disorder.

From Gladness to Purpose

I was always a chubby kid—athletic, to be sure, relatively quick for my size, and much more flexible than most teenage guys. I had killer definition in my calves (and still do, for those of you keeping score). While I didn't like how I looked (and it was pretty clear to me that most potential dates didn't either), as a budding defensive lineman in American football, my size was beneficial. I still remember the joy I experienced the first time I burst through the offensive line and crushed the opposing quarterback, a middle schooler who didn't yet have the benefit of a hormone-driven growth spurt. I'll also never forget the dejection I felt after tearing ligaments in my knee and hearing that more football was possible for my future, but so was not walking if I continued to play the sport. Not wanting to permanently injure myself or lose the ability to walk, I stepped away from football. Suddenly, without the one purpose that made my size and weight seem worth it, my body seemed worthless.

So I began to lose weight. I changed my diet and started a love-hate relationship with cardio, particularly stationary bikes. By the by, one of the workout secrets I discovered as a middle schooler still works to this day: find an immersive video game, play that while you're riding or running, and don't you know it, the time passes quickly. Doing this over the first year, I dropped from a high of about 265 pounds to about 185 pounds.

People took notice. People were impressed. I received praise from my skinnier, more conventionally attractive peers, something that felt quite rare. Not only did my body seem more wanted by romantic partners, but my family was also proud. My parents and grandparents alike gushed. Basking in their affirmation, I too was proud.

Proud, but not satisfied. My goal weight was 165 pounds, a full 100-pound drop. And that 185 weight was a plateau I just couldn't break through. If vocation was tied to gladness, and everyone in my life was so thrilled with my weight loss, then surely I needed to keep the process alive. I'd experienced the high of near-universal affirmation, which made me feel like I had a purpose—getting skinnier and hitting my goal weight—that was worth any risk.

As a sophomore in high school, I started vomiting after meals and taking ephedrine pills to speed the weight loss. Eventually, I hit my 165 goal. And nobody knew, at least not at first, how I did it. No one except for me. Whatever I was, I was no longer proud, and my gladness was slipping away, meal after meal, pill after pill, year after year. Bulimia became the outward expression of my body image issues.

Keeping off weight lost in such an unhealthy manner is almost impossible without unhealthy practices, so for years I continued to throw up after each meal, sneaking away at Thanksgiving to the bathroom, always turning on the exhaust fan to cover the sounds of the retching. For years I continued to take diet pills, seeking salvation in supplements.

Over time, I noticed I was constantly lightheaded. Traveling with a Christian band between high school and college, I passed out during the first set of one of our youth events in Denver. A flurry of studies—EKGs and EEGs and MRIs and CAT scans and PET scans and blood tests and sleep studies—all finally confirmed a constellation of diagnoses. An arrhythmia, a heart condition not alien to my family but certainly exacerbated by years of ephedrine and puking, compounded by chronically low blood pressure and low blood sugar, each of which were complicated by the inconstant calorie consumption my body could expect on any given day.

All of this out of a pursuit of gladness. When I aligned my pursuits solely with chasing feelings of happiness or joy, I lost myself in search of those feelings rather than seeking out purpose beyond myself. In fact, part of my problem was the dogged chasing of gladness, but the other part was my self-absorption. I lost sight of the truth in Buechner's quote, the part of vocation connected with the world's deep hunger. In my obsession with weight loss, I didn't think about what was good for others. About how my behavior affected my community. About how my unnecessary personal risks also needlessly put others at risk.

This all changed when I began to pursue wellness rather than a particular body type. And that could never have happened without the intervention of loved ones who saw how deeply I was hurting and realized that my weight loss was tied up in a desperate pursuit of validation. An intervention staged by two friends, who happened to be ex-girlfriends of mine, set the stage for recovery. They weren't really friends with each other, but each knew deeply the pain I was feeling because of our history together, so they overcame their differences and our pasts to demand that I seek psychological help to confront my eating disorder. That moment was the beginning of my journey to wellness because they, much better than I, understood vocation. They did something that didn't include a lot of gladness, reconciling with each other to address me in my illness, in order to give me a chance at a more abundant life.

We are not called first to gladness. We are called first to purpose. When I defined worth based on gladness, and my gladness was tied up in the attention of others and the achievement of goals, I developed unhealthy practices, thinking that the emotional misery and physical damage were worth it. What I came to realize, though, was that my single-minded pursuit of weight loss wasn't one of vocation because I was focused only on myself and my feelings. True vocation considers the intersection of our purpose with the world's needs.

Defining Vocation

What my friends did for me was reveal that vocation isn't always about making yourself feel happy. It is about serving a purpose beyond ourselves. That's something I've come to experience quite clearly as a pastor.

As an ordained minister, I've been called to do some really difficult things. Counsel people facing addiction. Protest in the streets, during a pandemic, against anti-Black violence. Comfort children forced to undergo custody hearings amid family separations. Pray for people who just lost their jobs. Counsel families who experienced the sudden death of a child. Support people who experienced abuse. So many difficult things. Perhaps obviously, not one of those things made me glad. I felt no happiness, pleasure, or contentment. In fact, each one of them made me feel discontent. Each one revealed that the world is not as it should be, that deep needs in the world remain unmet, and we're called to meet them.

And yet that's precisely what made the work a part of my vocation. I was called alongside those people to accompany them in times of great need because in such desperate circumstances, no one should be left to suffer or struggle alone. To be a companion for people through strife and success is a holy endeavor, not only because it prevents loneliness, but because it also evokes shared purpose. For instance, there's a rush of energy in protests, a comradery in gathering to confront the reality of evil and hold society accountable to live differently. During the summer of 2020, I took part in multiple protests after the murders of George Floyd, Breonna Taylor, and too many others. Under the leadership of Black and Brown organizers, we gathered to face the terrible evil of racism, and amid that suffering, we also found an embedded purpose that energized us all. Because when the world is not as it should be, we're called to come together and realign toward what's right.

Don't get me wrong; there are certainly times that I feel gladness as a part of my journey. I love to preach and teach. I feel incredibly alive with a guitar in my hands, leading a congregation in song. Baptisms, especially for adults, bring a serene moment in the thin space between earth and eternity where I feel connected to all that is holy. Perhaps nothing makes me more joyful than witnessing my students take hold of their own vocations with conviction. There is a portion of gladness within my vocation for which I am deeply grateful.

But those joyful things aren't my vocation any more than the sorrowful or difficult things. Vocation is more than how we feel while we meet a need. We find our vocations in the alignment of our daily lives—careers, family, friendship, and citizenship—with the sacred purpose that gives life to all creation.

If I'm going to challenge a giant of vocation like Frederick Buechner, I need to provide an alternate definition, a different way to conceive of purpose. As I said in the introduction, I define *vocation* as "any meaningful, life-giving work you do for the world." Since this is a new definition, I'll come back to it frequently. By *meaningful*, I mean something full of integrity, value, or purpose. By *life-giving*, I mean anything that promotes human flourishing rather than threatens physical, mental, spiritual, relational, or environmental health. And I promise I'll talk more about that specific definition. Just not yet.

First, we must realize that as a calling, vocation comes from outside of ourselves. The word's origin hearkens to this outside-in nature of vocation, for the Latin root word, *vocare*, means simply "to call." To have a vocation is to be called from outside yourself. It isn't something we simply muster up and decide is worth it in the isolation of our minds. If we determine what's valuable in a vacuum, we disregard the input of so many other people whose perspectives matter. In their different approaches, other people share wisdom that's beyond our knowledge, experience, or tradition. Consider this: Many religious traditions emphasize that each person carries a divine image or a sacred spark. As I understand it, that means others carry a different part of God's image than I do. As do our neighbors and strangers, people like us and unlike us. Inviting other perspectives to reflect on our vocations welcomes more of the sacred into our story. To decide what's meaningful on our own dismisses the sacred wisdom carried by other people whose perspectives shine on the divine not obvious within ourselves. To state this another way, any definition of vocation that only arises from within is incomplete because it doesn't recognize our connection to the world in which we live.

Even so, while a calling comes from outside, that doesn't mean we should disregard what's within. The call from outside us awakens something inside us. As I work with college students, I see them come alive when their life experiences intersect with an internship that challenges them, or a mentor who supports them, or a service opportunity that inspires them. When the call from outside collides with a person's values, that's where vocation arises. Exponential value appears not because they're suddenly glad but because they've found ways to make meaning for themselves and give life to others.

People may sing different sets of notes that sound fine on their own. Yet when layered together, they either soar in harmony or collide in cacophony. The experience of vocation is the discovery of harmony, distinct notes of human activity that fit together and produce meaning they could not have produced on their own, creating harmony, a sound impossible in isolation from other voices singing the song of purpose. We experience vocation in community because something from outside calls to us and harmonizes with the deepest parts of ourselves.

Who Is Calling?

Of course, a calling implies a caller, a voice or an agent outside of ourselves. Who calls you? Who is it that does the calling in our lives?

In my tradition, vocation is tied to God's call in our lives. God calls us to action that is meaningful and life-giving for the world. Too often, though, that's been a difficult concept for many to grasp because there's no predictable way to hear the voice that calls us. Christians believe Jesus, God embodied, ascended into heaven about two thousand years ago. Since then, with the notable exception of mystical visions, nobody's seen the guy, much less heard him call. Not even a text!

Except, of course, that's not the whole story. When Jesus ascended, he also sent the Holy Spirit, God's life force, to live within humanity. That, combined with our belief that everyone bears God's image, means that we still hear God speak. It's just not in the voice of a two-millennia-old

Palestinian dude (though admittedly, I really wish I could
have that conversation). I'm so grateful that I hear God calling through Black Lives Matter protestors who seek a justice
that rolls down like a waterfall. I hear God calling through
my niece's voracious love of wildlife. I hear God calling
through Capital University's Interfaith Student Organization, a community of religiously diverse practitioners who
find common bonds in our humanity and help one another
appreciate the varied practices we present. To paraphrase
a hymn that my grandmother dearly loved, God truly does
speak to us everywhere. God calls us through myriad voices
as the sacred permeates the universe.

In what ways, I wonder, is God calling to you?

The importance of that question is the reason this book
relies on more than just Christian teachers. Though Christianity gave birth to the concept of vocation, it's not real
estate that we own. Vocation points to the holy presence
and holy purpose possible in *every* life. I've learned about
this presence and purpose from Hindu priests and business
owners, Jewish rabbis and community organizers, Buddhist
monks and teachers, Muslim imams and students, atheist
physicians and farmers, agnostic factory workers and sec-
retaries, Jain teachers, Sikh scholars, and yes, a multiplic-
ity of Christians—all of them friends and none of them
more important than the other in the process of vocational
exploration.

While I say God, others might say Allah or the Lord.
Twelve-step recovery programs acknowledge a Higher
Power. Still others might say Wisdom or the Universe. Brahman or Sophia. Common humanity. The Great Spirit. Life
force. Something beyond us, something cosmic, is calling
us. It's that call's blending with our own voices that creates
the harmony of vocation. It's the purposeful collision of the

interior and exterior that, like the big bang, spins off new forms of life and new possibilities for growth.

To embrace your vocation is, in a sense, to live and work in ways that consistently align with the sacred force that calls to us all. As you begin to explore your vocation, consider the teaching from Zen master Dōgen, a thirteenth-century Japanese guru: "If you are unable to find the truth right where you are, where else do you expect to find it?"[2] Truth, enlightenment, wisdom, purpose, even holiness are present with us now. The practices of this book, especially the later chapters, are designed to help you access those transcendent realities, become more mindful of your present situation, and inhabit a purpose that matters to you and others. The call to our vocations comes from outside ourselves, but not just in mountaintop highs, feelings of gladness, or even moments of profound clarity. The call comes to us through the experiences we have, the communities we inhabit, the relationships we develop, the scripture we study, the media we consume, the activities we undertake—truly, our entire lives. Every moment can shape our vocational journey, for God can and does truly speak to us everywhere and in any thing.

Empowered to Answer

You are called from beyond yourself. There's a sacred voice calling to something holy within you. And here's something significant about your calling: you have the capacity to respond to your vocational options. No one, especially no heavenly being, forces you to make a particular choice. You have the power to choose your response to the calls in your life. Sometimes that call comes with social expectations, like being a citizen or a family member, and sometimes it's the choice of whether you undertake that vocation at all, like a marriage or a career. You have agency to determine what your vocations are and how you perform them.

This opinion is certainly unpopular with some religious folks. I know that because they've told me so! In their eyes, there's only one possible path that fits God's plan. To be honest, I understand that line of thought. Many people are taught that God or destiny determines their future and that no matter what they do, they can't change that trajectory, and so my sense of choice is just a mirage. They've said, for instance, that God predestined me to be a pastor, and there was nothing that I could do about it. But I'm not convinced that is true. I have had lots of opportunities to politely decline possible vocations—or at times, run in the other direction.

For instance, my grandfather Frank Tucker started a small business in 1960, a meatpacking plant that eventually became a slaughterhouse and grocery store that's been in the family ever since. By the time I began forming memories, my grandfather was retiring, handing over the day-to-day business to my dad (Terry) and uncle (John). At this family shop, I entered my first job bagging groceries. I eventually graduated to stocking shelves, to the lunch meat counter—even to wrapping and cutting meat. I've got the knife scars on my hands to prove it. I even got my hand caught in a conveyer belt once! (I have to admit, though, that one day on the slaughterhouse floor was enough for me.)

I learned a lot throughout that time: how to work hard, how to be a good colleague with people different from me, the complications of running a small business, the importance of feeding people, the integrity required to continue to provide insurance and retirement benefits as big-box stores squeezed more and more of the market share, and yes, the importance of keeping your limbs outside of heavy machinery.

I also learned that this work, though absolutely meaningful and life-giving for others, wasn't to be my vocation forever. While feeding people is certainly noble work, I didn't draw the kind of cosmic or even communal meaning from that job that my father did. Terry Tucker is rightly known by many in Wayne County, Ohio, as "The Butcher" because that vocation was so clearly his call until another blessed call, that of retirement and grandparenthood, called in a new direction. This vocation of butcher was also, just as clearly, not my call, because I couldn't wait to do most any other kind of work. That doesn't make working in the food industry a less holy vocation. It simply makes it not my vocation.

I know others whose choice to pursue careers outside the family business wrecked family relationships, but fortunately, neither my dad nor Uncle John put pressure on me or my cousins to take over the business. Now one of the cousins runs Marshallville Packing Company, a smaller, leaner version of the business formed after we sold the slaughterhouse to Smucker's. Yes, the jelly people. Their international headquarters is in the same industrial park as the former location of Tucker Packing Company, and as they expanded to produce coffee, pet foods, and other revenue streams, they needed more space as we downsized. My family discerned that with one person instead of two running the business, we couldn't operate at the same efficiency or effectiveness as before and decided to reorganize in order to fit the call on my cousin Jim's life.

This possible call, this potential vocation, came from outside myself, from someone—my father—who has more clearly exemplified God's image in my life than most people. Yet I said no. Not because it wasn't good. Not because I didn't appreciate his hard work, or John's hard work, or Grandpa Frank's hard work but because that work strained more than it supported my sense of purpose. I struggled to find meaning in the way others did, and so I pursued other possibilities. I said no to one thing in order to say yes to something else.

My tradition, Lutheranism—in particular, the Evangelical Lutheran Church in America—talks about the internal and external dimensions of God's call. That's where our ability to say yes or no comes from. An external call unmatched by an internal response does not in fact point to one's vocation. Similarly, an internal desire unmatched by an external force does not define one's vocation.

Now, this gets complicated because there's a difference between feeling and call. That's at least one reason Buechner's definition is insufficient. For instance, new parents will tell you that there are days, more than most would like to publicly admit, where they don't feel like getting up in the middle of the night to change, feed, or comfort an infant. Yet some combination of biology, social responsibility, and sheer will moves them, day in and day out, to do what's necessary to support that child's life. There's an internal meaning that drives them to perform well even when they don't feel like it. That's what I was missing at Marshallville Packing—the drive to participate in and make meaning when I didn't otherwise feel like it.

Another misconception about vocation is that there's only one vocation for each person. This often creates fear about choosing the wrong vocation. There's this anxiety that there's only one career that's right. One marriage partner who's perfect. Or only one living situation that's best. But here's the thing: we all hold multiple vocations at the same time. I'm a pastor, for sure, and also a professor, an author, a mentor, a spouse, an uncle, a godparent, a citizen, a child, a sibling, and so many other things. These are all vocations. They're all ways I engage in meaningful, life-giving work for the world. More than that, while we hold multiple vocations, there are also multiple ways to find meaning as a spouse, or in a career, or through citizenship. This journey of vocational exploration is like a prism through which the single beam of light passes to display an array of beautiful, divergent colors, all of which came from the same light source. None of those refractions are more or less a part of that light. As long as we choose vocations that are meaningful to us and life-giving to others, then we choose to act in the light of vocation.

That choosing might seem daunting because, well, it's a lot of responsibility. But it's also a holy gift meant for us. There's not simply one way to make meaning in the world, and not each of these life stations lasts forever. Like seasons of the year, so too vocations can change, which means we have many opportunities to find meaningful and life-giving work for the world. Rather than a chance we might miss, vocation is a journey we can always undertake.

So, then, how do we begin to understand what our vocations might be? How do we identify the options and opt into the process? That's where 4D Formation comes in.

4D Formation: Discerning the Call from Beyond

If you're called from beyond yourself, it makes sense to ask how you can develop an internal appreciation of your call. That's where the process I've developed can help you not only comprehend but actively claim your vocations. I call it 4D Formation.

I'm a science fiction nerd. Even as a child, I was enthralled with the possibility of life beyond the three dimensions we know so clearly: length, width, and height. Many forms of science fiction speculate about the fourth dimension, the dimension of time, since we seem so unable to control time, even less than we can control our own height, length, and width. Diet, exercise, shoe lifts, even surgery can change our first three dimensions. But we cannot control the speed by which time passes. We cannot redo time. There are no mulligans or do-overs. Time, it seems, is beyond our control.

Which, of course, is why I'm in love with the idea that we're time travelers. Sci-fi explores the possibility of us engaging time in a different way. Comics like *The Flash*, movies like *Avengers: Endgame*, series like *Star Trek* and *Stargate*—all of them speak to this sense that while time seems so constant, we might have more influence over it than we imagined. The movie *Interstellar*, for instance, builds on the theory that gravity affects time. Other shows play differently with the understanding of time. The *Doctor Who* franchise imagines that more specific control over time travel is possible, with the Doctor and their companions showing up at predetermined points across time and space. Just imagine being able to relive the mistakes, to fix all the wrongs! But wait—even the Doctor admits that there are certain fixed points that simply cannot be changed.

Science fiction isn't the only realm that has considered the possibility that we're time travelers, though. Lutheran theologian Wolfhart Pannenberg argues that Jesus was a time traveler, and in his mysterious, divine ministry, Jesus invites us all to join the journey across time and space. Pannenberg even gives this theology a super cool, comic-ready name: *futurity*.

In *Theology and the Kingdom of God*, Pannenberg makes this point: when Jesus said "the kingdom of heaven has come near" (Matt 4:17), that wasn't just an analogy.[3] Christians believe that in Jesus, the fullness of God is present. In Christ's presence, nothing separates humanity from divinity, so time-bound humans encounter the fullness of God's timeless presence. How fantastic is that? With God's presence comes God's reign. Eternity appears within time. Wherever God goes, there heaven is. And so with Jesus's incarnation comes Jesus's realm. Heaven shows up in the person of Jesus. In a wibbly-wobbly, timey-wimey way (you're welcome, Whovians), Jesus travels through space and time to bring the fullness of God into our space and our time.

So when Jesus invites people to participate in the reign of heaven's nearness, such a summons is not just a rhetorical analogy; it's a real, tangible invitation to travel to the future through the present heavenly door. To live a Christlike life is to travel to heaven. To embrace our purpose, to live out our vocations, to perfectly reflect eternity in the present time. This is time travel because it brings the future into the now and brings contemporary people a moment of the future's holy perfection.

Another connection between science fiction and our calling is worth considering. Just as time is beyond our control, so too vocation seems beyond our control. Just like vocation, time comes from outside of ourselves and places a call on our lives. Sometimes discovering a vocation makes us feel like we're characters in *Interstellar*, with a force pulling on us with such great strength that time passes in otherworldly ways. At other times, we feel much more in control, like we're flying the Doctor's TARDIS. And yet, however we experience vocation, it is all a part of something that comes from beyond that invites us to travel within a purpose greater than our own, even as it recognizes our own purposes as holy too.

The four dimensions of 4D Formation aren't the same as those that guide physical life in the universe. Instead, they're practices of exploration that help us time travel to engage our vocations with eternal consequence in ways that bring heavenly meaning and heavenly life to earth right now. Vocational exploration is the interwoven process of discovery, discernment, development, and decision that guides us into the sacred purposes of our lives. Later chapters dive deeply into those four dispositions and give concrete examples of how to discover our options, how to discern our values, how to develop our skills, and how to decide our next steps on this journey.

First, though, we need to focus on a key distinction, one that can literally save lives: the difference between vocation and identity.

Chapter 2

Defining Our Terms

Every semester I meet with multiple students who are quite distraught because they've realized they need to change majors. This isn't an abnormal situation for college students; in fact, at least one-third of college students change their major once.[1] But rather than understanding the shift as an opportunity to recognize their calling, some students see it as an identity crisis. Sometimes this distress arises because the student always imagined themselves as, for instance, a vocal music teacher—until they realized during their field placement in a local school that they love music but don't love working with children. Other times, external influences such as families place expectations on students that don't match the student's passions, purposes, or talents. I've seen parents pressure students to become lawyers when the students have no interest in law or doctors when the students have little scientific skill. Combine this experience with a rise in mental illnesses such as depression and anxiety, and students feel lost in themselves and like failures to their community. One summed it up this way: "If this isn't my major, I don't know who I am anymore."

Such thinking isn't unique to college students. Consider adults who experience career changes. Of course, when someone is fired, fear sets in about the ability to meet immediate needs, such as food and shelter. Yet more than once I've heard a peer who's lost their job ask a question similar to the one my students ask: "Who am I if I'm not working?" This could be "Who am I if I'm not working as a teacher, or as a musician, or as an athlete?" You can gain or lose abilities, which either prevents you from doing the work you once did or compels you to do some other work. Acquiring a temporary or permanent disability might require a shift in how you do a particular job or lead you to change a career. Acquiring a new set of skills or credentials might mean your employer asks you to take on a different role. In each situation, I've heard people wonder, "Who am I if I'm not doing X?"

We also need to keep in mind that vocation isn't only about what we're paid to do. Shifts in life stations—those roles we fill in social settings—can evoke similar responses. Parents whose children leave for college or move into their own homes lament what's commonly called "empty nest syndrome," the experience of not knowing who they are without their children around. When someone's parent dies or someone loses a spouse, whether through death or divorce, that person might question their identity without those familiar people as a routine part of life. As abilities or responsibilities change, so does how we spend time as volunteers or in recreation. When a career or relationship or habit change leads us to question who we *are* on the other side of that change, there's a good chance we're missing the distinction between vocation and identity.

Part of the problem in understanding the difference between identity and vocation is our language. In English, we use the verb *to be* to claim both identity and vocation. I just as easily say "I am a straight, white, cisgender, invisibly disabled man" as I say "I am a pastor, spouse, and US citizen." Yet those first terms are identity markers, while the second are vocations. If we don't clarify that our vocations are not our identities, a loss of vocation can seem like a loss of identity. Our identities are related to our vocations, to be sure. But people young and old will benefit from understanding the distinction.

So how do we differentiate between vocation and identity? *Identity is who you are. Vocation is what you do.* Our identities remind us that we each retain sacred worth, no matter our capacities, gifts, callings, and stations. Our vocations remind us that in every season, our lives have purpose, as do the lives of others. These ideas are related, to be sure, but they don't mean the same thing. *Worth* and *purpose* are not synonymous. Let's first explore the notion of identity, then note its similarities with and distinctions from vocation.

Identity Is Who You Are

In my tradition, when we baptize, we emphasize that our first identity is as a child of God. In this way, baptism reminds us of the sacred worth within all humanity, one first given in creation and brought to new life in baptismal waters. Other traditions call this worth a divine spark, holy breath, or shared humanity. From sages across the globe and wisdom throughout the ages, this commitment rings forth: our identities are always of sacred worth, for our value is set. We are holy and wholly beloved.

Identity is who we are before we do anything—the essence of our being, the way we exist in the world for ourselves. This isn't selfish, though it might sound that way at first, nor does it ignore a divine origin or a social community. Instead, it recognizes that our identities are deeply personal, the cores of our creation. Identity is who we know ourselves to be and how we make sense of our existence. People of faith recognize they are connected to and dependent upon a transcendent being, a sacred life force. Because identity is grounded in a divine image, it is constant. Before we go to work or have children or vote in a local election or bring a casserole to a sick neighbor, we exist in belovedness. Even as the world changes around us, even as our bodies change, even as our work changes, that sacred worth remains. I often assure college students that their worth is not the sum of their worst mistakes and best successes. Rather, they're beloved before they act and remain so at the conclusion of every work.

A confluence of factors—including race, gender expression, sexual orientation, ethnicity, nationality, ability, family of origin, and others—shape our identities. In this mix of nature and nurture, who we are is formed socially, influenced biologically, and for Christians, grounded liturgically in baptism.

That our identities are socially formed means external factors—over which we have limited control—influence the identities we claim. For instance, the language we're taught to speak first, and whether we're taught subsequent languages, instills in us a communal identity and limits (or expands) our ability to communicate outside of that community. We're born into our ethnicities, which are rooted in our families of origin and our locations. While we can expand our horizons, the culture in which we're raised as children is most likely to remain our primary point of cultural reference throughout our lives.

That identity is influenced biologically refers to a range of factors, from our natural abilities to skin color, that are products of our own DNA. Much like our social formation, we have limited control over our biology. We can augment

it, but we cannot prevent it. As someone who takes manufactured serotonin (antidepressants) daily, I personally
experience these limits. An invisible disability, my identity as a person with depression arises because my body
produces insufficient amounts of chemicals to balance my
moods. The medicine I take limits those effects, but it does
not erase my depression entirely. In other words, my identity doesn't change, but I can better comprehend how that
identity impacts my life and manage its expression.

Underlying these social and biological factors is a theological truth: we are beloved children of God. This aspect
of identity is deeply personal and yet originates outside of
ourselves. To be a child of God means to be created, to be
dependent upon a creator, and to have an intimate relationship with that being. In particularly Lutheran language, we
affirm that "God claims us" in the waters of baptism, restor-
ing the image of God given to all people in their creation
through the death of sin and the resurrection of the new person, reflecting Jesus's death and resurrection in the Gospels.
All other identities, all other ways we know ourselves, are
built upon this essential worth, this constant core value that
belongs to each of us. You, in your race and your nationality
and your family and your disabilities and your sexuality and
your gender, are of wondrous worth.

Of course, it's still possible for our understandings of
identity to shift. Consider, for instance, identities related
to physical abilities. Someone might identify as a "temporarily abled" person, acknowledging that a time will likely
come—whether due to age, accident, or illness—when
disability will become a part of their identity. Many other
aspects of identity can't be changed, however. We can't
wake up one day and simply decide to change our sexual
orientation, our race, or our ethnicity. We do sometimes

become more aware of the truth of those identities or make choices to more accurately present our identities. I think, for instance, of my friends and students who have transitioned with gender-affirmation surgery. While some might assume that's an identity choice, that's not how they've described it to me. They tell me they've made a decision to change the physical characteristics of their body to more naturally align with the gender identity within them.

Vocation Is What You Do

While identity is who we are, vocation is what we are called to do. If we can trust that we are of sacred worth—always—then we're freed to explore vocations that fulfill and even amplify our identities. That's one of the reasons this definition of vocation starts with meaning. Our sense of meaning connects to our identities, to those things truest about ourselves. And how we define *meaning* is also connected to our values, which we will explore in later chapters. But for now, think back to the distinction between things that make us glad and things that foster meaning. Sometimes things are meaningful—that is, they serve a purpose that is important to us—that don't bring us joy. Even without joy, the underlying purpose makes this work worth our effort.

Still, our vocation is not predetermined. We ultimately choose our behaviors, our investments, our work. But all too often, people confuse vocation with identity, and that can be destructive. A faithful pursuit of vocation, then, must clearly distinguish between the two.

One simple way to think about this is this: identity reflects your worth, while vocation reflects your purpose. Sometimes, because of my station in my family, I'm called to do certain work that I don't particularly enjoy. This could be anything from changing diapers or taking the garbage out of the house; to teaching my parents, yet again, how to work their smartphones; to giving the eulogies at my grandparents' funerals. Those are very different examples, but trust me, none of them leads to gladness. Yet they are meaningful because they enhance my family's wellness. Of course, my family would love me even if I didn't do those things. But because of my identity as a Tucker, born into this particular clan of English, German, and Irish immigrants to North America, I choose to express that identity through certain kinds of work on their behalf. In other words, I inhabit those vocations in ways that are connected to my familial identity. Yet if I stop being a pastor or can't figure out a problem after the latest smartphone update, my inability to provide assistance in the ways I have before doesn't mean I've lost my place in the family. It simply means the way I live out that vocation will change.

For many of you, the idea that we can separate who we are from what we do is laughable. Here's the thing: you're not entirely wrong. There is certainly overlap in who we are and what we do, but again, they're not the same thing. Consider this Venn diagram, two partially overlapping circles (figure 2.1). One circle stands for your identity and the other for one of your vocations. The overlapping area is where vocation and identity seem like the same thing because the synergy is so strong between the two. It's understandable that we've lost this distinction because much of our lives happen in the overlap between identity and vocation.

One result of our living in this middle ground is that when we receive feedback for something we've done that is primarily about our vocation, we take that as a comment on our identity. Whether this feedback is praise or blame, it can

Figure 2.1: *Identity and vocation*

reinforce the conflation of identity and vocation. This confusion can lead us to question our identities when in fact we should be exploring our vocational options.

We experience the distinction between identity and vocation in other arenas. For instance, part of my job requires administrative oversight. As many of my colleagues will attest, administration is not my spiritual gift. It's not something to which I'm predisposed, it's not something with which I strongly identify, it's not a natural tendency of mine. Yet due to my role on campus, it's something I'm called to do, so I work hard to get better at it in order to best live out my vocation. Just because we live much of our lives in the area where the circles of identity and vocation overlap doesn't mean the circles are the same.

In other words, sometimes we're called to labors that are important for our vocation but not rooted in or essential to our identities. *Essential* means something is of absolute value and tied to the essence of our being. Trust me: monthly credit card reports are *not* essential to my being. But they are *important* to my work—that is, to be a good steward of the money that comes to our ministry from student tuition, from church partners, from alumni donors. That's necessary work, even if it doesn't connect to the deepest parts of my identity. In this way, we can express identity through vocation, even if parts of a vocation don't feel joyfully related to the core parts of ourselves.

My vocation as a son also reflects this distinction. When my parents die, my vocation will forever change. I will still be their child, and my identity as a Tucker will not change with their deaths. But my actions certainly will. I'll no longer work to support their physical lives, though my efforts will hopefully further the positive aspects of their legacy as I work in society through things like charitable giving and community organizing. You, too, will experience change in your stations in arenas like family and citizenship. The changing nature of our stations in life is one reason it's so important to understand the difference between identity and vocation. If we don't understand that our value remains as our work changes, we can spiral into despair when a person leaves, whether by death or by choice.

Too often, we either lose our identities in our work or lose our work in our identities. For instance, if when I say "I am an author" I mean my identity is that of an author, what happens to my identity, the core of my being, if I never write again? I might feel like I've lost myself or that my existence is meaningless. But if I understand authorship as one of my vocations, an absence of writing doesn't mean an absence of myself. Instead, no longer writing is a change in my work, or even my purpose, but not in my identity. That's a different kind of shift, one with its own difficulty, but not one that challenges the nature or value of our existence.

The distinction between our vocations and identities not only preserves our sense of self-worth; it also frees us to live with fuller purpose through our vocations. Think back to the image of the prism. It's valuable in itself and casts light without effort. Yet if you shift the prism, the refractions change. The substance of the prism casts light in new ways because of the different way it is positioned. So, too, we remain who we are no matter what work we do. Through different actions, we reveal different parts of our identities, which shine different parts of the divine.

Once we realize that our worth does not depend on our work, we are freed to work with specific purpose in particular arenas. We no longer carry the weight of the universe on our shoulders. We can realize in our deepest selves, beloved by God before we do any work, that it's not our job to save the entire world. Instead, through meaningful, life-giving work for the world, we participate in God's mission through the specific callings in which we participate.

Communal and Personal Implications for Mental Health

We can't, or at least shouldn't, talk about identity formation and vocational discernment without addressing the plague of mental illness that impacts all people, especially youth and young adults. All too often, my conversations with teens and twentysomethings reveal that their mental health struggles cause them to question their identities, worth, and purpose. Evidence of such struggles is not limited to my ministry. Recent research reveals that between 2009 and 2017, depression increased in kids aged fourteen to seventeen by at least 60 percent, with rates rising by nearly

50 percent among those between ages twelve and twenty-one.[2] Even worse, after a period of steady decline in the early 2000s, suicide rates among preteens and teens nearly tripled between 2007 and 2017.[3] In fact, more than half of those we lost to suicide during that time had not been diagnosed with a mental health condition.[4]

There's no single reason for this devastating rise in mental illness and its related loss of life. Netflix's 2020 documentary *The Social Dilemma* argues that social media play a central role in creating feelings of missing out; in fact, a few years ago, the acronym FOMO—fear of missing out—became a popular term to describe this common experience among young people.[5] Media personalities blame different factors, including the internet for its ease of access to violent, prejudiced, extremist information; the easy availability of guns and drugs; increased pollutants in our air, food, and water; a decrease in closeness among biological families; and many others.

While researchers can share the haunting reality of mental illness and suicide, data cannot pinpoint a single explanation for the causes. Neither am I suggesting a single, or even simple, solution for mental illness. Neither clarifying our identities nor discovering our vocations is a certain solution to the suicide epidemic. Deeper self-awareness will not cure mental illness. But understanding the value in our identities and the purpose in our vocations can offer hope.

I know the profound importance of this distinction not just because of the growing evidence that student success (defined by increases in students' average grades, graduation rates, and self-reported appreciation of education, among others) correlates to students' discovery of purpose through formal and informal education (through what educators call high-impact practices) but because of my own story.[6] For me, mental illness and suicidal ideation aren't abstract ideas; they're a part of my journey in understanding my identity and my vocation.

My journey with bulimia, which I talked about in the previous chapter, came from a deeper-seated depression, one that was diagnosed in the midst of the academic rigors of graduate school. You see, I had conflated my identity with my intelligence and connected my value with my competency. I'd graduated as a salutatorian from my high school and earned my bachelor's degree summa cum laude, "with highest distinction." If they give you honors with a different language, it's supposed to mean more, right? Sadly, I bought that narrative. I swallowed that Latin pill.

When I failed my first Hebrew Bible exam at Duke Divinity School, I was devastated. I thought my life was over. I judged my worth by my ability to earn a certain grade, and that grade was a lot higher than an F. I believed my value was defined by my academic performance. When I came face-to-face with the reality that I wasn't as smart as I thought I was—and that I certainly wasn't the smartest person in the room—then I drew a different conclusion, steeped in error: I believed I wasn't the person I thought I was. I thought I'd lost my identity.

What I didn't realize at the time was that this crisis had been building for my entire life. As a child, my parents would find me holed up in a closet, reading by only the light of a flashlight. I couldn't verbalize my seven-year-old inner monologue, but even then I was overwhelmed by the pressure to perform academically. So to give myself a chance to enjoy reading rather than to be critiqued because I wasn't yet doing it perfectly, I hid from the world. No one could tell me I was mispronouncing words if I was by myself.

No one could quiz me on my comprehension if I was in isolation.

Years later, my body-image issues and depression collided in a violent, virulent eating disorder that infected almost every relationship I had. The struggles I faced with romantic relationships throughout high school and college pointed to a deep inner despair. I sought the approval from others that I could never find within myself. Bulimia and other forms of self-harm, including unsuccessful attempts on my own life, were the physical evidence of my undiagnosed, untreated mental illness and its connection to my evolving identity crisis.

When I first sought counseling after that most fortunate of interventions by my friends in college, it was focused on the eating disorder, and I was careful to not let any conversation veer too deeply into issues of identity and the depression I struggled with because of who I thought I was (and wasn't). I wasn't interested in dismantling the dysfunctional scaffolding that supported my semicharmed life. I truly believed the solution to the pain under the surface was earning external affirmation for my academic performance. But years later, that first failing grade, though a relatively small thing, threw that delicately balanced dysfunction off-kilter. Fortunately, I was more equipped at that point to recognize this dysfunction and truly get the help I needed. I sought a new counselor at Duke who finally gave names to what I'd been experiencing: clinical depression and generalized anxiety disorder.

I found this diagnosis ultimately liberating. It didn't solve the issue of a failing grade—paying better attention in class and more humbly listening to classmates did that—but the name for my struggles opened a possibility for me. I have sacred worth, not despite my disability, but within it. I can work to better understand that part of me and manage how it impacts my life, but that doesn't make me more or less beloved. Once I saw that, I also saw that my vocational failures didn't detract from that value, nor could vocational success inflate my value. In this distinction, I found a new way forward, one that could intentionally evaluate my work without devaluing myself.

Identity as a Prism for the Holy

I know I'm not alone in this struggle to differentiate between identity and vocation, nor am I the only one to experience the pain and danger that come with such confusion. Throughout my ministry, I've met people whose entire identities seem to be wrapped up in one particular vocation, like mine was with academia. Too many times I've seen an unexpected change in someone's vocation lead to an identity crisis. In turn, this often begets unhealthy behaviors and unnecessary risk taking. For instance, think of a student athlete who loses a starting role on the team and then parties the night away before the big game instead of preparing to support the team as a reserve. Think of midlife crisis stereotypes, such as driving a sports car too fast, outspending one's means, or adopting extreme social shifts like isolation or codependence.

Such destructive behaviors often arise when a change in work, not only career but work with family or friends or community, leads someone to question their worth—a conflation of vocation and identity. But when we see that identity is not lost or lessened when our vocations change, we can gratefully embrace the truth that our value continues despite the end of that vocation. When a vocation is no longer ours, we do not lose our worth. When our vocations change, we remain beloved, by God and by others, because our identities are more than what we do. Identity is the core of our very being.

While in graduate school, I read a book called *Refractions* by Makoto Fujimura that forever changed my perspective on truth and identity and inspired my fascination with prisms. Fujimura, a Japanese American painter who connects art, faith, and culture in his work, introduces the metaphor of refraction to create a bridge between his art and his experiences as a New Yorker in the immediate aftermath of September 11, 2001.[7]

In physics, refraction refers to the way a prism breaks one beam of white light into a multitude of colors. A prism, though usually glass, can be any transparent material. Depending on where you are in relation to the prism, you'll see different portions of the refraction. And the type of prism and its position in relation to the light source will cause it to refract light differently. This means that you won't ever be able to see all possible refractions at the same time, and as you shift around the prism, moving from place to place and seeing the different colors and shapes that cast through, you can perceive different and unique refractions of that one light. This is why no two people ever see the exact same rainbow. From their perspectives, the light appears with varied splendor. To more fully comprehend the light cast through a prism, multiple people can observe the light from different angles and share those perspectives with one another. We, individually and collectively, can also use different prisms to see the different ways the same light can be refracted. For Fujimura, just as his physical artwork refracts light differently depending on the type of mineral in the paint, kind of light, and position of the viewer, the essays in his book offer different perspectives on beauty and suffering in the world around him as he witnesses to life in the wake of 9/11.

Here's what I love about prisms: They don't go to work. They don't activate. They don't try. They simply exist. The light passes through them, and voilà—a beautiful new perspective on the other side without a hint of effort by the prism. That's the beauty and wonder of your identity. You are a prism for the holy. Long before you act, whether in a relationship or as a citizen or at a job, you are sharing the holy—refracting sacred light—simply because you exist and the sacred shines through you. I tell my students that each of them refracts a necessary and beautiful part of God's image because they reveal something divine that I could never see without them. Each of them acts as a different kind of prism, uniquely displaying something holy to the world in which we live. Because we are the work of the holy, we reveal holiness simply by being ourselves.

This metaphor also helps people of faith appreciate the goodness of a pluralistic world. Even though we understand and relate to the divine in a particular way, we can acknowledge that somehow, some way, all people refract the divine. Some people struggle to see such diversity as valuable, believing their perspective is right while others' is wrong. Because we can't see the fullness of any rainbow cast through a prism, our views can be myopic—that is, narrowly focused on us. Since we can't see the truth from someone else's point of view, we tend to think difference is evidence of ignorance or falsity. But if each of us is a prism that recasts the same light in different ways, then difference doesn't communicate something wrong. Instead, it shows just how many ways goodness can flow through us and how together, by sharing our perspectives on the light we see, we can come to understand the wonder of the light more fully.

If we can acknowledge that each of us brings something sacred into our global and local communities, then we can enter interreligious relationships with humility. This is true not only for religious diversity but for healthy relationships with people who are different from us in many ways.

Your identity is who you are, and through that identity, you refract the light in wondrously unique ways, making the world shine better because you are here. Before you ever discover your purpose or work, you have absolute worth. In an era when self-esteem issues run rampant, when depression and anxiety like I experience plant insidious lies within our heads and hearts, we can together uphold the value of each and every person as a compelling counter-measure. Like an antiviral treatment that surrounds a virus with medicine to counteract the illness, the compelling truth that we are God's beloved and of inherent, inestima-ble worth surrounds the lies of worthlessness and prevents the sickness from spreading. Such a safety net allows other influences—those of medicine and pastoral care, of clinical counselors and healthy coping mechanisms—to inspire this holistic, authentic sense of self-worth in us. A change in work might shift your perspective and the light people see shining through you, but it doesn't demolish the prism that you are.

More Abundant Life

I'll say it one last time because it's that important: Iden-tity is who you are. Vocation is what you do. To distinguish between identity and vocation matters deeply because, ulti-mately, it is in the dynamic relationship between the two that we can find abundant life. When we embody the distinction between identity and vocation, we live the fullness of life the creator meant for us.

I take the words of Jesus seriously. His whole purpose, his vocation, is for all people to have life and life abundant (John 10:10). My faith tradition understands Jesus's life, death, and resurrection as meaningful to God and life-giving to all creation; that is, Jesus inhabits a particular vocation. Rather than using *abundantly*, the New International Version translates the Greek as "to the full." The interplay between identity and vocation is not about only us as people. It helps us properly see the connections between who God is (identity) and what God does (vocation). Specifically, we learn who God is because of what Jesus does. Jesus's example establishes for humanity, each of us divine sparks that we are, a way to faithfully reflect our identities without confusing them with our work. Understanding the difference between vocation and identity is not just a theoretical concept or philosophical divide; it allows us to integrate vocation and identity without conflating them because, in essence, to live our vocation is to put our identities to work in different ways, ways that can change without changing who we are.

As you come to understand this distinction, you might develop another fear. If your identity is different from your vocation, what about all the parts of you that are hurting or incomplete? How can any of us be called to holy work with the failures of our past? Fortunately, when God calls you, you are called with the fullness of yourself, integrated into the particular vocations that are yours to take up. You need to hide nothing of yourself as you carry out your calling because, after all, it is *you* who God calls.

Chapter 3

You Are Called Wholly

Identity is who you are. Vocation is what you do. Personality is how you express who you are in what you do. And God calls you to your vocations as a whole person, leaving none of you behind.

Every so often when discussing purpose with college students, one will say something like "I couldn't possibly be a pastor with all of my sin." Others will say, "Well, I'm passionate about teaching art, but I'm really good at math, so I need to do what I'm best at, right?" I even hear, with some regularity, that one failed test or one challenging experience means they must change their entire career trajectory. These questions and doubts are common among not just young adults but people of all ages. While they make sense to many, there's something wrong with this logic. Our past failures don't necessarily prevent us from future vocations, nor must our talents become our careers. Whatever we're called to, God calls us with all of our identities, experiences, and abilities, not despite them.

You are called with the fullness of yourself. This means that God calls you with your strengths and weaknesses, your abilities and disabilities, your experiences and naivete, your assets and your needs. You don't need to be perfect, whatever that means, to live out your purpose. Rather than demanding perfection, living your callings takes commitment.

Martin Luther, a theologian from the sixteenth century who ignited an era of reform in the church, wrote that we're simultaneously sinners and saints.[1] For Luther, this meant that while all baptized Christians fail to completely embody God's holiness, God in holiness still loves and accepts us. God sanctifies us sinners, which makes us saints even amid our sinfulness. Following this logic, baptismal vocation is not evident in perfection, because we're not perfect. Instead, the commitment to meaningful, life-giving work in the midst of imperfection reveals a divine presence in our lives. We can and should apply this thought process more broadly. Every human carries a divine spark. Every human also makes mistakes. We each have significant limitations and vast potential. None of us is perfect, and yet all of us are called. We can't wait until we achieve perfection in order to inhabit our purpose, or else we'll never activate our vocations. This is true of every person in every time and place. God calls us with something: all of ourselves. The holy calls us wholly to our vocations.

Evolving in Calling

Realizing the ways that this call to vocation operates in our lives is a lifelong process. Sometimes we feel unsuited or ill fit for particular vocations, but that doesn't mean it's impossible or improper for us to consider those opportunities. Perhaps you've read this common piece of vocational wisdom, memed by many across social media: "God doesn't call the equipped. God equips the called." Let's not just accept it at face value, though. Of course, God calls us with a certain skill set we can use to accomplish specific goals. God calls us with experiences that fit the needs of future situations. The talents we bring will, at times, fit the exact needs of a community we're called to serve. So yes, God doesn't ignore the innate talents we bring to the table or the passions in our hearts.

People also grow into callings, however. We may find over time that we need to learn new skills or express different talents in order to meet emerging callings. God equips us through these experiences of growth, which we talk about at length in the chapter on development. Pauli Murray exemplifies this progression.

Pauli Murray may be the most significant person who lived in the twentieth century whom you've never heard of.[2] She/he (Murray chose to use male and female pronouns at different times) certainly has made a profound impact on my life and on my sense of vocation. Murray embodied several vocations throughout life, including lawyer, activist for Black and LGBTQ+ rights, organizer for the National Organization for Women (NOW), and poet. Across decades of activity, Murray responded to God's call with a willingness to learn new skills and deploy new tactics to meet the needs she/he felt called to serve. Murray sometimes used he/him pronouns and at other times used she/her, sometimes referring when speaking and writing to an inner maleness and outer femaleness. At all times, while dealing with those external influences and internal tension, Murray fought for equal rights for all people. Murray didn't view experience as determining possibilities. Instead, Murray found that the divine call reshaped Murray's vocations. Case in point: after the death of Murray's longtime partner, Irene, she/he entered seminary and in 1977 became the first Black woman ordained as a priest in the Episcopal Church. God called Pauli Murray as a lawyer, an activist, an organizer, a poet, and eventually as a priest with the fullness of identity, background, and experience, including the things that didn't make sense to others and the growing edges Murray would need to develop. And in a wonderfully unique set of identities, Murray found meaning in each of those callings.

What I came to know through Murray's witness is this: we're called with our identities, experiences, and abilities, not despite them. God calls us as whole people. If you have questions about who you are or how you might fit potential vocations, that's OK. God is still calling you. If others question your fitness for the work, that doesn't mean God's not inviting you to try. If you don't have the skills or the training, there's still time to learn and practice. God calls the equipped *and* God equips the called.

That we're called wholly to our vocations could sound like bad news, at least at first. If you're unsure of yourself or question your capability, you may not want to bring the fullness of yourself to your calling. You might feel embarrassed or unfit. I struggled with such questions and feelings for a long time. With my mental illness and eating disorder, I felt insufficient to meet the vocations available to me. I felt unworthy. I felt like I had failed in the past and that such failure would determine my future.

But that God calls us as whole people is not bad news. It is good news. First, it's good news because, remember, you are beloved by God and called to sacred purpose. Your value has been determined, because in God's estimation, you are inherently valuable. You are worthy and worth the effort you need to put forth to live out your vocation. Once I realized that, I found myself empowered by the Spirit to learn new habits, to develop healthy coping mechanisms, and to rely on others to strengthen me in my weaknesses as I seek to live a meaningful life that is life-giving for others.

Paying attention to who we are, the self whom God calls, can help us clarify our callings. For instance, it can remind us that we're not called to everything. Not every opportunity we encounter is a fit for our experience bank, skill set, passions, abilities, interests, or willingness to grow and learn. Because of that, part of our assessment of potential vocations includes weighing the possible callings against those that may be meaningful for us. The realization that we're not called to everything can free us from any sense of obligation to fix all the world's problems and instead allow us to focus on those things closest to the intersection of our priorities and God's priorities.

Recognizing we are called with all of ourselves also reveals which vocations are not ours, those that are likely the callings of others because of who they are. For instance, as an author, I'm much more of an idea and content person and not so much of a grammar and format expert. Because of this, my wife, Michelle, has read almost every meaningful paper I've written since we began dating, since one of her many vocations is that of an editor. Combine that with the excellent work of my team at Fortress, and you get this book. My limitations don't prevent publishing. Instead, they reveal where I need to rely on others' vocations in order for all of us to more fully live out our purpose together. I live out my calling more fully and more faithfully when I recognize and support others in their callings.

Which leads to this point, perhaps the most important of all: since we're called with all of ourselves, we're called together. Our vocations don't exist in isolation. Your callings, based on your strengths, help address my weaknesses. As your vocation enables you to manifest your abilities, you meet needs that I, with my inabilities, couldn't. Vocation is work done for the world—for others who through their vocations fulfill roles in our lives as we through our vocations fulfill roles in theirs. If we're going to do life-giving work, we need a community in which to live that more vibrant life. We'll talk more about this in the next chapter, where community is the center of our conversation.

Finally, and more personally, when God calls us as whole people, sometimes we notice vocations that intrigue us but don't fit our current skill sets. That experience points to opportunities for growth. A strong sense of your value empowers you to consider what changes might be necessary for you to embody this potential vocation. Like Pauli Murray, you may experience the end of a relational vocation that inspires a new journey, like a return to school later in life. You might seek a mentor to offer guidance for your development. You might hire a coach or counselor to help you practice particular skills and apply them to specific situations. The potential to grow requires that we make ourselves vulnerable. Though likely uncomfortable, as we recognize that our identities and our vocations are not the same, growing—which flows out of our value rather than challenges our worth—can be an invigorating process.

Personal Development for Vocational Exploration

Growth is not about only developing skills and talents, however. In the best sense, exploration of your vocation can also inspire personal development. Perhaps your experiences make you comfortable in a specific context, but you need to adopt certain skills or behaviors to apply that vocation more broadly. Or perhaps you have a certain gift that you could share with others, but you need experience to learn how you might share it effectively.

Imagine, for instance, you're a talented artist and considering becoming an art teacher. Being an artist is one vocation, and being a teacher is another. It may be that both flow from your identity, but that's not necessarily true. Especially if you were a prodigy, you've long been aware that not everyone is as talented as you are. Teaching art means you must learn how to train others to use skills that came naturally to you, and training others means you must learn skills not just in art itself but in pedagogy, in psychology, and in other fields. This doesn't detract from your vocation as an artist but instead reveals that the vocation of a teacher might require some development. In this process, called as a whole person, you bring both your talents and your needs to the process of vocational exploration.

The need to grow in order to take hold of a calling can be daunting. To feel so called to something and realize that you lack the requisite skills right now might even feel damning. But that doesn't mean you're not called to that work. Instead, it means to inhabit that call, you must respond with all of yourself, not just your skills but also your limitations, and submit them to the possibility of growth or the potential for change. Recognizing the need for growth and education in order to better inhabit your calling reveals a commitment to your vocation, not a failure in your identity.

Conversely, if you're not willing to make the changes necessary to embrace a possible vocation, that also reveals something valuable. Perhaps this call, at least shaped in this way, isn't for you. Per the earlier example, not all artists are called to be art teachers. Some have a vocation as professional artists. Some continue art as a vocation through hobby or charity but not as a career. That's been my path.

My vocation as a musician is not how I make money or even spend most of my free time, even though it is meaningful for me and (I hope) life-giving for others. Sometimes I find meaning in songs I write—serious or silly—for my family and church communities. Sometimes I find it behind a drum set with friends, remembering the fun we used to have as a band years ago. It's still a vocation of mine, though not a career. This vocation isn't ultimately a way to make a living or even something I want to share widely; instead, it is a way for me to share who I am that brings laughter and inspires reflection for a smaller group of people.

Because you are wholly called, you may find it difficult to bring certain parts of yourself to your vocation. We might hold back rather than admit failures or acknowledge a lack of experience or skill. At other times, we might hesitate to assert ourselves because others have devalued or denigrated parts of our identities or histories. None of those challenges necessarily disqualifies us from a vocation. Instead, they can invite confession, critique, repair, and growth that prepare us for incredible work in our call. Sharing our whole selves in safe ways reveals the relationship between our identities and our work.

We should not ignore the intimate connections between our identities and our vocations, because how we express our identities will shape how we inhabit our vocations. Our gender and sexual orientation and race and other identity markers, along with our personalities, will impact the way we live our purpose. Unfortunately, some use others' identities as reasons to prevent qualified people from living into their vocations. For instance, many Christian churches refused to ordain women for way too long, mainline protestant churches took even longer to ordain Black women, and all churches took even longer to ordain LGBTQ+ people. Their identities were used to preclude them from valid vocations where their work could have been meaningful and life-giving for all involved. While people like Pauli Murray break glass ceilings, overcoming such identity-based prejudice is still a struggle for many. Even though you know God calls the equipped and equips the called, this does not mean the world around you will readily accept that truth. Even so, never forget that your work to claim your vocation is worth the intentionality and effort you put forth.

Sharing your whole self certainly entails risk—but also great opportunity. The ways you've fallen short might lead to not only confession but also forgiveness and opportunities to repair damage done. The parts of you that others have written off might be revealed in the fullness of their beauty, vitality, and relevance. Sharing your whole self is emotional labor, to be sure, but doing so confirms to both yourself and others the valuable connection between your identity and your vocations.

So how do you pursue your call with all of yourself without losing your way? The rest of this book is concerned with that question. I suggest practices, some you can do on your own and others that require a community. The entire process of 4D Formation, in both concepts and practices, ultimately honors the whole person you are as you engage in vocational exploration.

One of the most significant aspects of vocational exploration is that you don't have to do this work alone. One of the best practices I've found to help comprehend the fullness of myself—successes and failures, skills and shortcomings, assets and debts—is working with a spiritual director (which some call a spiritual companion). While the experience can feel similar to clinical counseling, spiritual direction is not therapy. Spiritual direction certification doesn't qualify someone to diagnose or medicate others for psychological afflictions. Instead, a spiritual director accompanies the directee on their journey of self-discovery. Rather than give answers, spiritual directors are good company on a treasure hunt to help unearth the perspective, knowledge, and awareness that's buried somewhere within.

Spiritual directors accomplish this through regular meetings or retreats with directees and primarily employ two modes: listening and questioning. While a spiritual director will offer appropriate feedback when asked, spiritual direction focuses on you, your thoughts, and your wisdom. In the cacophony of noise so present within twenty-first-century life, where we so often must compete with others to have our perspectives heard, a spiritual director carves out space to listen to you and only you. Your spirituality, your struggles, your confusion, your excitement, your purpose are the topics at hand. Rather than set a path to healing or wholeness, a spiritual director helps you more deeply commune with the divine and explore what that connection means for your life, including your vocations.

When you come to a place of resistance in that process, a spiritual director asks questions. It's important to note that there's a significant difference between questioning and interrogation. A good spiritual director is not a detective, perhaps accusing you of some specific behavior, but instead an inquisitive student of your life, curious about how your personal experiences and connection with God might equip you to face the obstacle at hand. Once, in a conversation with my spiritual director, I found myself at a barrier I couldn't overcome. I'd been lied to by someone in power at work, intentionally misled in ways that devalued my vocation. Hearing the despair in my voice, my spiritual director simply asked, "It sounds like their values of your company are making you question your value as a person. Is that true?"

Like a river bursting its dam, my tears flowed. While I knew cognitively that there's a difference between my identity and my vocation, the devaluation of my vocation led me to doubt my worth as a person. In the hectic reality of higher education, I lost sight of the difference between myself and my work. That line, too easily blurred without a system of support, was lost.

What a spiritual director can do is provide you with an invaluable partner to help you ground yourself in your values, whether from a religious or secular worldview, when challenges inhibit your journey. If you're interested in securing a spiritual director for yourself, Spiritual Directors International (https://www.sdicompanions.org) is a great place to start. Thanks to the advent of video calling, many spiritual directors—including my own—meet directees online, so the opportunity is more accessible than you may realize. Yet if you have trouble finding access to a spiritual director, consider asking a trusted mentor or peer to listen nonjudgmentally. You can even undertake an open-ended journaling process that begins with a simple question like "How is it with my spirit?"

While spiritual directors empower us to recognize the resources we have within ourselves and the deep well of the sacred within us, sometimes we meet challenges that require something different. Whether through education, treatment, or medication, a clinical counselor, psychiatrist, or physician can provide access to resources we don't have within ourselves.

Using appropriate medical resources is vital because not all problems we face are conceptual or internal struggles. While I failed to differentiate between my identity and my vocation, my body also didn't produce the proper balance of chemicals to foster a stable state of mind. Just a few milligrams of manufactured serotonin daily helps establish a biological baseline for my mental acuity. Along with care from a counselor or physician who can help coach you with coping mechanisms and provide resources for holistic wellness, this level of investment can help you clarify your identity, in its fullness, as distinct from your calling, even as it contributes to your vocations.

Finding, Creating, and Interpreting Maps

You are called wholly to this holy journey. A map is a valuable tool that helps most journeys be successful. When explorers set out on a new journey, sometimes they bring others' maps with them, and other times they become cartographers and create maps of the environments they encounter. Exploring your vocation is no different. Some maps, created by others, will help you discover, discern, develop, and decide your purpose. And sometimes, you're going to have to describe the landscape, draw the boundaries, and even critique others' maps.

These vocational maps aren't found in atlases or apps. Instead, we find them in the biographies—including written stories, videos, and personal conversations—of those who've lived our vocations before us, whether auto technicians, civil engineers, dairy farmers, athletes, artists, or some other role. I learned how to be a spouse from good spouses. I learned how to be a pastor from good pastors. Their stories reveal the steps they took to learn and grow, and in many ways, I have followed those steps. We learn our vocations in part from those who've come before, and in the coming pages, there are suggestions for particular ways you can experience others' vocations as a way to map out your own possibilities.

But just as you're uniquely you, these veteran explorers are uniquely themselves too. Their maps won't fit 100 percent with your life, and that's a good thing. You will bring things to the journey that they never had, and they will have used resources not available to you. When you read these maps, know that you're going to have to redefine some things for your life, at least insofar as they relate to your potential vocations.

Because others' maps do not necessarily perfectly fit your journey, interpretation is a necessary part of vocational exploration. Maps might not work for us because landscapes change, sometimes suddenly due to fires, floods, tornadoes, and hurricanes and sometimes slowly due to erosion from rivers and tides and even the flow of glaciers and the disintegration of ice shelves. Over time, rivers change course. Fires burn away entire forests. Glaciers move mountains. Hurricanes change coastlines. Perhaps the vocational maps you're handed need to be redrawn because cultural change has opened new routes of travel that were unavailable to those who came before you. Technological developments may render their directions out of date. Just as the world map has changed due to shifting national borders, so too your vocational map might change as organizations start new initiatives, cease operations, or become more relevant as your journey progresses. In short, always ask whether the maps that you're given match your experience of the terrain.

When we encounter things in the landscape that don't appear on the maps we're given, we sometimes need to redraw the chart. Sometimes this change is necessary because our identities, along with our personalities, skills, and talents, are different from those of earlier cartographers. At other times, we need to make changes to the map because the vocation itself and the environment are different. To be a carpenter in the twenty-first century is different from doing such work in the first century. With transformations in tools, the advent of electricity, and changes in available materials, the landscape has changed for many vocations. Politics in the United States look very different today from in the days after the Revolutionary War. Voting today happens on electronic machines, whereas in earlier eras, paper ballots were filled out by hand. Votes in the first elections in our country were cast in a public forum by voice rather than by secret paper ballots. The environment has even changed for friendship. Technological developments in cell phones, internet connectivity, and global mobility have changed the ways we connect with and support one another. Once, friendships were typically bound by geography, but now with immediate communication technology, some of our most meaningful relationships can span the globe.

Finally, though, let's admit that not all maps are good maps. When Europeans first came to North America, explorers' and settlers' maps suffered because they ignored the wisdom of native peoples or simply didn't pay close attention to their own experiences and so produced documents showing that Florida wasn't a panhandle or that California was an island. Clearly, those maps were wrong and needed to be redrawn. Similarly, while I've learned much about how to be a pastor and a spouse from those who came before me, sometimes I've learned what not to do by examining the maps left by others whose examples are less than exemplary. The pastor who yelled at staff in public for disagreeing with him taught me very clearly what an unhealthy leadership style looked like. The embattled spouses who refused help when offered by friends and professional counselors showed me how the poisonous combination of fear and pride can ruin a marriage. Those maps showed a path I didn't want my vocational exploration to take, and so I drew new boundaries that better fit my identity, defined new landmarks that better served the needs of the people I'm called to serve, and charted a different course toward a healthier form of vocation.

We must always be reassessing the maps at our disposal in order to ensure they accurately reflect the reality we engage. That's true of our physical landscape, and it's true of careers, citizenship, and friendship. So because of differences in us and differences in the vocation, we can't simply follow the maps that we've been given. We've also got to start defining the landscape as we see it and defining the path as we travel it.

Stars

Part of exploring our vocations is looking down at your map, and another is looking at the landscape that surrounds us. But what happens when we lose ourselves on the landscape and the maps are no help? Bringing the fullness of ourselves to our vocations involves looking within and looking ahead but also looking up to the stars. In nature, the stars are one tool we can use to orient ourselves on our journeys. The sun, a star, rises and sets, both marking time and providing light for our journeys. Ancient travelers navigated at night using stars to point them in the right direction, with the North Star serving as a constant reference point for wayfarers in the Northern Hemisphere. The constellations, even as they shift with the seasons, are stable guides amid changing landscapes and new terrains. Even when clouds temporarily cover them, the stars remain. Just because we can't read the stars at the moment doesn't mean they've disappeared forever.

What, or who, are the constants in your life? These are the things that constitute the metaphorical stars in your vocational exploration. For me and other people of faith, God or some transcendent reality acts as a North Star. For some, groups of people, like families, form constellations that shift with seasons but still help orient them. For others, core values offer guideposts as they plot their daily journeys. Because maps are sometimes unreliable and because landscapes change, watching the stars is essential to any successful journey, including your vocational journey. At times, the maps you employ will fail you. At times, the ground you travel will shift beneath your feet. When this happens, look to the constants in your life like sailors would look to the stars.

Part of your work in vocational exploration is to identify your stars, the constants that guide you when all else fails. When you can clearly identify those, you can orient your journey to align with the priorities they mark. If you haven't developed a clear sense of your purpose, then you might begin by developing a mission statement. Another way to identify your stars is to assess the fundamental aspects of your faith and how it relates to your experience. Still another is taking note of the people who remain consistent in your life—family of origin or of choice, mentors, friends, even adversaries—and noticing how they relate to one another and to you. These constellations of purpose, faith, and persons can become indispensable parts of your journey because, when all else fails, they remain.

We're drawn to the stars not only because they're constant, though that's certainly helpful, but because there's a profound connection between the stars and us. After all, we're made of stardust. This isn't a metaphor. Literally, the constituting elements of your body were formed in stars millions and billions of years ago. Supernova explosions sent these minerals across the universe, comets and asteroids crashing into moons and planets throughout the cosmos, including earth. That fundamental mixture of life's building blocks that shape your DNA, your brain chemistry, your melanin, your smile, your personality—it all began in the burning gravity of a star. Humans have been looking up to the stars throughout our evolution, seeing something of ourselves in the far-off galaxies above.

To name your stars is to highlight the most authentic expressions of yourself and their connections to these cosmic constants of your journey. To identify the stars in your vocational journey is to make clear the connections between your core identity and the inspiration you find in your purpose, faith, and other people. Like the constellations above us, our vocations complement the vocations of others in ways that create a new mosaic, one that would be impossible without each of our contributions. Even when they're in motion, just as we are, together we complement one another, a network of pilgrims sharing information from our maps as we explore our vocations. When we find our map is insufficient or when we encounter a new landscape, we don't travel alone. We continue with the stars as our guide, inspiring our journey ahead.

You Are Called with the Fullness of Yourself

You are called with the fullness of yourself. Like Pauli Murray, you may find resistance to your identity, evolutions in your personality, and yes, changes to your vocation. Tools like spiritual direction and counseling can help you address those situations with confidence. Along the path, maps composed by others who share your vocation can serve as resources to develop your own map for your journey. When those maps fail you, or when a seismic change reshapes your environment, the stars in your life remain constant companions as you explore your vocation. We turn now to how this connection, in community, functions as one way that God calls you.

Chapter 4

Called through Your Communities

Who's calling and how? If a vocation is a calling, then it is appropriate to ask, Who speaks the words of call? Who signs the way to our purpose? Who writes the invitations to our meaningful, life-giving work for others? Of course, the easy answer is God (or some might say the universe), which is certainly true. But the primary way we experience God's call is through other vocational explorers, through our communities.

I don't mean to romanticize community here. Life together with people is often difficult. Different opinions, divergent perspectives, and competing priorities can create conflict within community. Such conflict may hurt us as our identities are attacked by a parent or our value is doubted by a peer. Not all community is safe community. Yet we can learn something from every interaction we have. That doesn't mean every person's opinion is accurate or every piece of advice is applicable to our vocation. It does mean that our vocation can be sharpened every time we meet another. Life in community can clarify your vocation, so let's explore more deeply how that might unfold in your life.

Embodied Community

We experience this holy call in at least three kinds of embodied community: family, civic, and religious. If vocation is any meaningful, life-giving work we do in the world, then it is a material matter. It's not materialistic—focused on the acquisition of things or the accumulation of wealth—but it is experienced in the stuff of our existence. That is, our vocations are formed and embodied in communities for the thriving of all creation. Our participation in earth's ecosystem is itself a spiritual activity.

It's important to understand that claiming our embodiment is not antithetical to acknowledging our spiritual essence. Many religious traditions see the spirit of God or a divine spark or a holy image at the heart of human existence. How that is expressed by various religious or spiritual traditions will differ. Some traditions see bodily life as a temporary state, while others see bodies involved in the next life, whether through reincarnation or resurrection. But at the core of this commitment is an awareness that we experience transcendent significance through our embodied lives. For vocation, this is especially important, since our purposes in the world relate to meaningful, life-giving work that benefits other embodied creatures.

We are called as creatures with spirit and body, both deeply grounded in the present and profoundly connected to the eternal. As embodied images of God, divine sparks within the stuff of the earth, we relate to other bodies in physical and metaphysical ways. We find our vocations by living in communities of creatures through whom we meet the holy of holies.

Because we are embodied creatures, other people, places, experiences, diets, movements, hobbies, living conditions, and so on—truly a whole host of factors—influence the way we experience our callings. Since few people, even religious people, hear God speaking in a direct and audible manner, the divine communicates with us through indirect means—our ordinary, embodied human lives. We learn something of holy purpose through a lover's touch, a stranger's smile, a child's laugh, a parent's tears, a coworker's skill, an artisan's craft, an athlete's movement, a singer's timbre, a poet's lilt. Each of these embodied experiences can speak to your vocation, or reveal something that's simply not yours, even as you might still appreciate its value.

Such experiences are part of what my tradition calls the external call. While I'll talk more about external calls in chapter 7, a few words are appropriate here. Our passions, interests, values, and convictions are ways we experience a call internally. We know we have identified our vocation when this internal call aligns with an external call—appreciation, affirmation, or commission that comes from outside of us. Our communities, through whom God calls us, are the agents of external calls. They are the voices, sometimes speaking in a whisper and sometimes through a megaphone, through which God inspires us to find purpose beyond ourselves yet connected to our identities. Discovery, discernment, development, and decision, which we will explore later, each includes aspects of both internal and external calls.

So in what kind of communities do we experience God's call? We often hear it first from those closest to us, our families.

Family

I use the term *family* broadly, not referring to only your biological family. I mean your family of choice, those people with whom you've made a life, the people you've chosen to significantly influence your life. Family might include a close confidant, a steady mentor, a financial advisor, an emotional web of support, or nearly any other person you allow to impact your daily existence. This might include your biological or adoptive parents and siblings, but it can also include spouses and extended family, godparents, a Friendsgiving crew, book group members, sports teammates, and support group peers. Family is the people with whom you choose to spend the best of times and the worst of times. This community—those closest to you, the ones with whom you choose to be vulnerable—becomes one of the most significant amplifiers of God's calls in your life.

We get a hint of the way family forms us—and the way God speaks through family—in simple matters, such as the connection between our families and our favorite hobbies or preferred foods. With a family meat business, I've certainly developed specific tastes and strong opinions about not only meat quality but the value of local farmers and butchers for both the workers' livelihoods and animals' quality of life. Similarly, while most of the men in my family have divergent athletic and artistic skills, most of us enjoy golf, also a favorite pastime of mine. For me, these preferences are about more than a taste for steak or a few hours of swinging sticks at small, round objects. They communicate values of justice and fairness, appreciation of physical activity and nature, an embrace of natural life cycles. Just because my family members cared about certain kinds of food and athletics didn't mean I was predestined to like those things, but the early and ongoing connections certainly made such preferences more likely. And this is only a small picture of the influence family can have on our values.

Social formation in family runs deep. This group teaches you to speak a native language as a child and reshapes your language over time with new phrases, just as you bring new language into the family. I learned to speak an English dialect common to moderately wealthy, rural white folks in Ohio because I lived with English-speaking, moderately wealthy white folks among fields where farmers annually rotated corn, soy, and alfalfa. Later, thanks to her overhearing certain 1990s television I consumed, my mom still says, "Whatever!" almost anytime someone clarifies a piece of information. Thanks, *Saved by the Bell.*

Language, along with food and hobbies, is part of what we usually call culture. Our first priorities reflect the dominant culture of our families of origin and then later the cultures we cultivate alongside our families of choice. The culture of our broader communities influences everything from clothing, music, and religion to what a family looks like and what jobs are appropriate options. The priorities we adopt, shaped by the culture around us, reveal our values. Our values in turn determine whether something is meaningful for us and how that thing is meaningful. We value communication in language that we understand, often connected to words and phrases our families use. We value foods that give us comfort, like Grandma's buttermilk cookies or Grandpa's ribeye steaks. We value activities that entertain us and others, especially those that connect us with positive familial experiences. And similarly, these values predispose us to certain vocations.

Yet predisposition is not determination. Our family experiences introduce us to a number of vocational options that brim with opportunity and present obstacles. The stories my parents read and songs my grandparents sang to me both opened a world to me and shut off other possibilities. Sometimes, this framing is accidental, and sometimes, it is very intentional. I doubt my family intended the frequent bedtime readings of *The Runaway Road* to spark a vocation of travel.[1] But for me, those early stories about the journey inspired me to seek opportunities through work, service, and recreation to experience new places. Conversely, I am certain the Bible passages we read were chosen to instill certain values in my life. For instance, creation stories from Genesis emphasized God's omnipotence, while political references from Kings and Paul's letters reinforced submission to political authorities. But so many stories were left unread and so much terrain left unexplored. For instance, I didn't discover the story of Elisha and the she-bears (2 Kgs 2:23–24) until college or the story of Mephibosheth (2 Sam 9) until graduate school.

Our families open to us certain possibilities even as they ignore or squelch others. While some paths seem very possible, others remain hidden until other people bring them to our attention. Just because you've never thought of forestry as a career or monastic life as an option doesn't mean they're impossible vocations for you. To know that something is possible, you need to first become aware of its existence as a possibility. Thankfully, such options appear as God's call comes to us from other kinds of communities.

Civic Community

One of those communities is our civic community. This is the combination of schoolmates, coworkers, neighbors, and others we engage in the daily activities of life. Our social networks, from country farming co-ops to urban community development corporations, open us to possibilities beyond what our families could ever offer, although even these civic cultures sometimes coalesce and other times collide.

When I was a young drummer, my family's musical tastes shaped the beats I'd play and the groups I'd create. Yet this foundation in Protestant hymns and mid-twentieth-century American rock met a whole new expression when teachers steeped in jazz and classmates enamored of rap exposed me to new ways I could live my vocation as a musician. This experience not only gave new meaning to my life; it also introduced me to new communities with whom I could create more abundant life. Similarly, my political convictions changed as I grew in relationship with people outside my immediate family. You have likely experienced similar transitions. Our values and preferences change as we consider the validity and fit of the values and preferences of our communities, especially those that are different from our own.

The structures of our civic communities also communicate values, which we must assess. For instance, the constitutional and capitalist foundations of the United States establish certain priorities for our society, at least in theory. We must interrogate those structures in order to understand the ramifications of those values. Consider this: While some point to the Constitution as a paradigm for equality, the original document granted the promised rights only to white, male landowners. Women were not enfranchised until the twentieth century. Article 1, section 2, clause 3 of the Constitution counts slaves, those "bound to service," as three-fifths of a free person and excludes "Indians," preventing their full participation in the promises of freedom and equality.

Consider, then, capitalism as a defining narrative for our lives. Our increasingly unbridled allegiance to capitalism has slowly but certainly made money the dominant metaphor for most things in our lives, at least in North America and Europe. We talk about "social capital" as a relational influence in our communities. We talk about "investing" our talents to create more favorable returns, such as increased skills or fame. We ask about the "cost-benefit" analysis of a given situation. We ask about the ROI, the return on investment, to make or justify a decision. Every one of these phrases originates in the principles of capitalism, which have now invaded most every part of our lives. Capitalism, rather than the stewardship of our resources, rules over not just our cash but our society.

We do not need to adopt these values as our own, however. We can examine how they play out in our personal lives and our communities and choose which ones belong to us. Think about how schools teach and what content is included in curricula. Consider what holidays your local, regional, and national government recognizes. What are the expectations around paid parental leave in your company? Each of these decisions, and many more, explicitly or implicitly communicate values that you then adopt or confront. Life in community reveals the callings in our lives—sometimes as we claim its values and sometimes as we recognize a critical need for social change. In conversation with our families and our society, we begin to identify our own values and assess where we fit in in the grand cosmic narrative. When values conflict, we can attend to yet another voice, that of religion and spiritual practice.

Another area of social encounter is coaching. To many, the word *coach* inspires images of athletics. This makes sense, given the popularity of sports throughout the world and the high profile of coaches in news and entertainment sources. But athletic coaches aren't all about whistles, buzz cuts, and yelling. In essence, coaches are trainers and teachers who help a person focus on and achieve a specific purpose. Some colleges offer coaches to help students achieve academic goals. Faith coaches provide advice for and encouragement in spiritual goals. Recently, there has been a rise in the popularity of life coaching as a distinct practice, different from a therapist, counselor, or advisor to help people pursue various life objectives.

Coaches aren't always the best performers in their fields; rather, they teach others to perform. Coaches train people in certain skills and hone their knowledge of a particular area in order to reach a specific goal—an athletic championship, a benchmark grade on a test, a certain GPA, admission to a particular school, or a certain job. Faith coaches can help promote prayer practices, worship habits, devotional commitments, and other acts of discipleship. Faith coaches can help us identify the spiritual nature of all our vocations if we open ourselves to that possibility. Life coaches will also help seekers synthesize these various goals and prioritize commitments, though without the explicitly spiritual lens of a faith coach.

Sometimes a specific coach is very helpful for vocational exploration. While not often called a coach, music teachers are coaches who can help people discover talents and develop abilities that might lead to a vocation in performance. Athletic and academic coaches offer the same type of guidance. And when questions of purpose arise, faith coaches or life coaches can be helpful partners to explore the potential calls in our lives and evaluate their meanings. No matter our goals, though, a coach is someone who can help us identify the ways we may be called and the steps we can take in order to pursue that calling.

Religious and Spiritual Community

Let's begin with a differentiation between religion and spirituality. Both are concerned with ultimate meaning but differ in their approaches to it. By *religion*, I mean a set of prescribed beliefs and rituals, most often practiced as a part of a community. When I refer to *spirituality*, I mean an approach to transcendent meaning without external prescriptions, one chosen solely by the practitioner. Of course, there's lots of overlap between religion and spirituality. Consider the Catholic who disagrees with the church's teaching on same-sex marriage, or the Buddhist who also happens to believe in a god or gods, or the atheist who draws comfort from the rituals of Jumu'ah prayer at the mosque each Friday.[2] Despite their religious (or nonreligious) commitments, they've made a choice personally to connect with the holy outside the beliefs or practices of a religious identity they no longer want to fully claim.

Within that overlap, people increasingly distinguish between the two, identifying as spiritual but not religious (shortened by researchers and others to SBNR). You might feel more comfortable with this designation. Many of the students I work with no longer identify with the religious traditions of their families but still seek connection with the divine and search for a way to do so that best fits their developing identities. Sometimes, these people stay SBNR for the rest of their lives, while others gradually adopt a new religious identity or, less often, return to their religious origins.[3]

Whether you identify with a specific religious tradition or embrace a more SBNR approach to transcendence, you most likely do so in conversation with others. Others play a vital role in shaping our beliefs. We learn from the wisdom others have gleaned on their journeys, and we learn from the failures that appear as fault lines on their maps. Even if you claim a radical individuality, seeking to limit the influence of other people, you remain in conversation with God or the divine or the universe. Your understanding of that higher power probably shifts as you engage other people's perspectives, even if they are not explicitly about the transcendent. At some level, simply the interaction with another person shapes what you value in your life. After all, vocation is something inside awakened by something outside, and you discover that in conversation with your community.

Whether we claim a religion or identify as SBNR, ritual likely has a role in our approach to the transcendent. It also plays a part in the process of vocational exploration. Both individuals and communities employ rituals that reflect and form their priorities. Ritual supports the development of a habit, a repeated behavior that reveals and strengthens our values. For instance, daily hygiene is a ritual that reveals that personal and communal health is a priority. Performing and listening to music, from worship services to punk rock festivals to street-corner saxophones, are rituals that permeate many cultures and reveal an appreciation of both art and artist. A consistent devotional practice, prayer time, or scripture engagement both reflects and reinforces that practice as a priority.

When we practice a ritual with other people, it forms shared commitments among us. In fact, there's a whole academic field called ritual theory that studies the ways social interactions shape beliefs, morals—even culture itself. Catherine Bell, a ritual theorist, explains, "Ritualization is the construction of certain types of power relationships effective within particular social organizations."[4] In simpler terms, people create or participate in rituals to communicate, reinforce, or challenge power dynamics in their communities. There's much more to the conversation than that, but that essential understanding of a relationship between rituals and what we value undergirds this entire discussion. Since ritual plays a key role in developing and reinforcing belief, I recommend people who are exploring their vocation regularly engage in religious, spiritual, or other intentional ritual practices. I've seen three practices prove vital to this process among my students: conversation with others, critical engagement with scriptures, and regular worship.

Conversation

Though it might seem strange to call it a ritual, conversation is a repetitive behavior humans use to make meaning. One of my students had a multiyear Snap streak on Snapchat with her mom because they valued that connection and conversation with each other. It shouldn't surprise you to know that this student gives high priority to her vocation as a family member. It is the reason she pursues a connection with her mom, and the daily connection reinforces the priority. A coworker of mine ritually calls a rotating group of people when they walk the dogs every night, reinforcing their vocation as friends. Even a weekly staff meeting is an opportunity to express and refine your vocation in that community.

From social media to small groups to leadership meetings, conversation can also be a vital process for vocational exploration. So as you explore your purposes, you can ask for feedback about vocational possibilities from people in your community whose opinions you value. If you're struggling with a conflict between your own values and those of your family or society, you can invite a trusted member of your religious or spiritual community to share their perspective. As you develop religious communities and, through them, identify spiritual priorities, conversation can help you develop an essential plumb line for evaluating your vocational possibilities.

Consider, for example, how conversation about the priority of human dignity (which can be drawn from religious traditions like my Christianity or nonreligious traditions like a friend's secular humanism) might inspire a more critical approach to the Constitution of the United States. The dehumanizing treatment of women, enslaved people, and Indigenous people baked into the original form may make you question how to apply or interpret the document today. Seen in this light, we might more clearly comprehend the relation between our own values and the values of our society—valuable information as we consider the vocations to which we might be called.

Not all conversation is so explicit or so deep, but that doesn't mean we can't learn from every engagement. Joan Tollifson, a Zen teacher, riffing on the wisdom of Zen master Dōgen, once wrote, "Every moment is the guru."[5] This mindful approach to life encourages awareness that each word is full of meaning, that each gesture is pregnant with wisdom, that Walt Whitman was right to write "I contain multitudes."[6] So every conversation presents an opportunity to ask yourself what values are present in your community and how those match with your own. That approach acknowledges the holy in all creatures.

Scripture

Of course, one source religious and spiritual people look to for values is sacred texts. For millennia, people have gathered around holy writings to discuss, meditate, pray, and deliberate. From the Bibles of Judaism and Christianity to the Vedas of Hinduism to Taoism's Daozang, sacred texts provide essential conversation partners as we pursue meaningful, life-giving work. Indeed, the concept of vocation was born from the Christian Scriptures. Paul, writing a letter to a young church in Rome, told this new religious community that God called them with God's purpose (Rom 8:28). I borrowed the term *life-giving* from Jesus, who says he came so that we might have life abundantly (John 10:10).

You might be wondering, if we can be critical of the Constitution, shouldn't we also approach scriptures with the same skeptical eye? Yes, we should. Because sexism, patriarchy, xenophobia, and a host of other oppressive biases exist within almost every religious scripture and, consequently, within most every religious tradition. Within my own tradition, people used—and sometimes continue to use—certain passages to support the oppression of women and at least tacitly support racism, genocide, and other hateful behavior. Left unchecked, these texts have been used by abusers in marriages, by people attempting to justify slavery and Jim Crow, and even by nations and states to support ethnic-cleansing agendas. Such values are abhorrent. A faithful reading of scripture is a critical reading of scripture.

But if they're so problematic, why engage with scriptures at all? Why use them for vocational exploration? Because they've been set apart by religious communities and viewed as foundational guides—in some cases, for millennia. Repeatedly, when people utilize scriptures to justify evil behavior, others use scriptures to combat or correct that behavior. That abolitionists such as Sojourner Truth and Frederick Douglass viewed the Bible as a source of liberation, even as white Christians used that very same Bible to justify the horrendous practices of race-based enslavement, reveals the potential for scripture to guide communities. That throughout history people continue to claim the Bible and other writings as holy texts and use them in ways that liberate rather than subjugate people shows the continued value of scriptures—reading them, using them as a resource for prayer or meditation, interpreting them, performing them—to the vocational discernment process.

Using scriptures is not without problems, but neither is it without value.

I often tell my students that the Bible contains a thread of abundant life that runs from Eden in Genesis to the new heaven and earth in Revelation. This thread, highlighted most clearly in the life of Jesus, provides a consistent anchor for readers as they stitch together their interpretation of Scripture. In this process, it's helpful to remember that in Christianity, Scripture isn't God, and to treat it as such is idolatry. Scripture requires interpretation to comprehend how God is at work in and through the text. That's why my tradition refers to the Bible as God's written word, a document that testifies to God's Living Word, another way we refer to Jesus. This distinction is a reminder that while Jesus is fully human and fully divine, the Bible is not fully divine. The text is inspired by God but communicated in a fully human manner, so it carries the biases of the original authors. So if other parts of the Bible conflict with this thread of abundant life or the witness of Jesus, we err on the side of Jesus and the call to give life to all, to reconcile all things. The recurring message of liberation throughout the Bible, especially those passages that some have used as weapons of hate or tools of oppression, consistently upholds God's love and calls us to respond in love.

To engage with the scripture of your tradition or sages of your spiritual practice is to engage with the collected wisdom of others who've walked this vocational journey before you. As I said earlier, sometimes you'll need to draw your own map rather than simply use ones employed by other vocational sojourners, so you need not accept everything you read at face value. Instead, look at the consistent themes of scripture and ask yourself how those priorities reflect and affect the priorities of your communities, whether familial, civic, or religious. See how your call relates to the scriptures you claim and how they relate to your call.

Worship

Finally, worshipping regularly provides a tangible connection to the intangible and transcendent source of our callings. To worship means to "ascribe worth," to indicate the value of something in your life by naming that value. Worship is itself a ritual, usually though not exclusively done in community. To worship alongside others strengthens our own sense of commitment to our faith, the object of our worship, and the community itself. It also helps us identify a community of people we can enter into conversation with as well as with whom we can explore scriptures. Worship in many traditions is, in fact, a kind of communal conversation around scriptures.

Worship is a wonderful example of ritual theory in practice. To commit to regularly worshipping something or someone else is a constant reminder of the good that exists outside of ourselves. To sing songs from authors across cultures and eras reinforces the importance of other people's perspectives on the sacred. But just as scriptures can be problematic, worship experiences are not necessarily all positive formation either. Sociological research presented in *How God Changes Your Brain* points out that people who pray to a God they understand as angry are much more likely to be angry people. Fortunately, the reverse is also true: people who pray to a compassionate God are much more likely to be compassionate people.[7] Regular worship has the power to shape your beliefs, your attitudes, and your actions.

Since worship is so formative, be intentional about how you worship. If you are looking for a change in your thinking, then make a change in your regular worship practices. If you don't typically attend services, try committing to regular participation for a season. If you're already a consistent worshipper, consider making a change in the style of service or the community. For instance, predominantly Black churches read the story of Israel's exodus from Egypt very differently from predominantly white churches, both of whom will read it differently from congregations of Latino migrants. Hearing that story read, preached, sung, and prayed in different contexts will shape your understanding in different ways. Even if you worship in the same place with the same people, renew your focus on the content and setting of worship. What does the architecture tell you about holiness? What emotions does the hymnic harmony inspire? How does reading a particular passage in a particular area on a particular day help you understand different perspectives on that scripture's meaning? And how might those arches and feelings and words shape you differently with increased intentionality?

I'm specifically talking about worship in community as an agent of calling. Of course, personal practices and individual pieties are also important for our faith and formative for our lives, but since we experience call through communities, the kinds of worship that are most informative for our callings come in conversation with others as we worship. Whatever ways you choose to worship to explore your callings, do so in community with others, for we're all exploring our vocations, and we all have wisdom to share for the journey. You are called through these communities—familial, civic, and religious—a mosaic of people who together depict a myriad of potential calls for your life. How can you whittle that vast matrix of possibility into a more manageable subset of potentials to explore? Once again, not alone.

Environment

One factor that affects all of these communities is the environment in which we create community. By *environment*, I mean the landscape, the geography itself, and the movement that happens within and upon that space, from migration and civil engineering to weather and social life. In fact, the people we spend time with, along with their respective families, civic commitments, and religious affiliations, shape an environment. But our environments also shape us. The landscapes in which we operate communicate values. For instance, a lecture hall communicates one kind of priority in education, one that privileges one voice as the source of authoritative knowledge, while a round table invites multiple perspectives and the cultivation of collective wisdom. Natural space often communicates a community's preference for one way of life, while manufactured space may communicate a different desire. A city with affordable, accessible public transportation communicates a different civic priority for certain citizens—namely, people experiencing poverty—than a town that requires personal cars for commuter travel. Life in a rural area cultivates a kind of community that is different from an urban arena, and in the United States, we also see how life in the Midwest shapes expectations that are different from those of people in the Northeast or Southwest for everything from food and manners to political preferences and career options. As our environments give shape to our lives, they inform our expectations, and they contextualize our values, which in turn inspire how we envision our call to work in the world.

We experience God's call to meaningful, life-giving work in our everyday environments, sometimes because we're compelled by the heavenly values within our settings and at other times because we're compelled to respond to hellish conditions. For instance, the development of Black religious traditions in North America is the manifestation of a communal vocation that gives meaning and life to people who were ripped away from their lands, their peoples, their communities, and their homes. Some chose to make Christianity their own, taking the religion of their enslavers and embracing the liberation content so often ignored or intentionally obscured by white folks. Others fused African religious traditions together, along with aspects of Roman Catholicism, to create voodoo and Santeria. Still others embraced a type of Islam as a form of resistance to Christian colonizers who used religion to justify slavery, racism, and oppression. At times, as people experience injustice or tyranny, they discover vocations of resistance through which they seek to transform their environments for the better.

At other times, though, your environment will emphasize the goodness of a vocation. For instance, while in graduate school, I entered a particularly stressful season. My work conflicted with my ability to take full-time classes, but because my wife and I married when we were both still in school, we needed any income we could muster. I sat down with the registrar, who shared a program with me that would allow me to get academic credit for my work and reduce my financial commitments. Though this reduced the amount of cash I paid the school, he saw my health as a higher priority than profit. His grace and commitment to an environment that supported student success, even in the face of resistance from others in the administration, made an incredible impression on me and confirmed for me a vocation to support students in higher education.

It's within our environments that we experience families, religious communities, civic networks, and various types of coaching. All these factors shape our sense of identity (who we are) and vocation (what we do). Through critical engagement with the ways we are shaped by our social locations, we can become more aware of how we're called to various vocations in our lives. But how do we know that the purpose we identify has meaning beyond ourselves, that it's worth the time and energy we might invest in its pursuit? How might the ultimate meaning of the universe, that foundational purpose, give shape to our distinct vocations?

Chapter 5

Called for Transcendent Mission

So far, I've emphasized that you are certainly called, that you're called from outside yourself, that you're called with all of yourself, and that you're called through your community. What I haven't done yet is tell you how to determine exactly what you're called to do. Sadly, this isn't IKEA, so there are no step-by-step instructions for assembling your vocation. But there are some concepts and practices that will help you discern your callings. That begins with understanding how your purpose is related to the meaning of all life. Yup. What you're called to do is connected with the very substance of the universe.

You are called personally. But that personal calling connects with a cosmic purpose, a transcendent meaning, that shapes and directs the individual vocations each of us practice. You're called for something transcendent even as you're called to specific work, and having a clear sense of God's mission and your mission can help you more clearly grasp your vocations.

This is another area where the language of external call can help you understand the significance of vocation. If you're called to something, not only is the call coming from outside yourself, but the ultimate purpose is beyond yourself. It's not up to you alone to accomplish all things or fulfill all needs. An external call awakens something within you that seeks to meet not just your needs but the needs of others. That's why vocation is life-giving not just for you but for the world.

A Mission Worth Serving

You may have heard the axiom that the whole is greater than the sum of its parts. This ancient idea was popularized with Aristotle's *Metaphysics*.[1] Metaphysics is the study of existence and of the things that we know exist. Now, you might wonder why I'm bringing up abstract concepts when the whole goal of this book is to make clearer the notion of vocation. A fair question. Just stick with me for a second.

Remember that I've already emphasized that identity, personality, and vocation are different things. Identity is who you are, personality is how you express who you are, and vocation is how you put who you are to work. Those are, in fact, metaphysical claims. That your existence, the very substance of your being, is reflected in your actions but not entirely defined by your actions is to say that you are greater than the sum of your actions or vocations.

Similarly, the meaning of the work that we do is not found simply in the aggregate of our shared productivity. Something that includes all of us and is yet beyond all of us binds together our work, gives it meaning, and directs its trajectory. I understand that something as the *missio Dei*, the mission of God.

The mission of God is not evangelism as it's commonly construed on busy street corners. God's mission is not to manipulate anyone into church membership, to force someone to pray a prayer before eating a meal, or to shame someone for their past indiscretions.

As I understand it, God's mission is to reconcile all things, an idea that comes from 2 Corinthians 5 and Colossians 1.

The word *reconciliation* is used in various ways in different religious traditions. In my context, it is the restoration of right relationship among all members of creation as well as between creation and creator. Reconciliation, then, requires repair of the damage done by sin, otherwise known as reparation. This means that all our vocations—career, care for family, citizenship, hobbies, and more—should contribute in some way to reparation or reconciliation.

Just because something is called *reconciliation* doesn't mean that it restores right relationships, however. For instance, some forms of "racial reconciliation" look to force racial minorities to assimilate into the dominant culture, a common expectation for multiracial churches in the United States. Too often, in the name of reconciliation, Black and Brown folks are asked to leave their racial and ethnic identities at the door in order to fit into the prevalent white culture.

Other faith traditions speak of similar concepts. A key goal within Hinduism is *moksha*, liberation from the cycle of reincarnation and into eternal unity with and awareness of Brahman, the substance of all creation. Similarly, Sufi Islam describes the experience of *fanaa*, a release from sin and absorption into a holistic relationship with Allah. These relational descriptions of ultimate existence suggest to me a kind of reconciliation, where all creation ultimately participates in unceasingly healthy relationship with its creator.

For all these traditions, the ultimate purpose of existence is beyond us and yet something to which we can contribute with our everyday lives. We can pursue healthy relationships today that reflect the kind of ultimate relationship we seek to realize. We can act now in ways that honor the sacred value of every person and every creature. We can live in ways that remind all people that every molecule of the universe has meaning within itself and beyond itself.

This transcendent meaning, which ties us all together, is the foundation of reconciliation.

Even so, you might understand the purpose of the universe differently from the way I do. What's important is to be clear about how you understand that transcendent mission so you can be confident that your particular vocations align with that cosmic purpose. So take a moment and answer this question: How do you understand the transcendent meaning of life?

Mission Partners

Often when we pursue our purpose, we can feel overwhelmed by the vast needs we see in the world. In the hustle and bustle of life in North America, simply the pressure to perform each day is crushing. We strive to earn the grade, secure the internship, win the position battle, get the solo, receive recognition, be the best—all because that's how we think we serve a purpose beyond ourselves. Sometimes the pressure is from the outside. Sometimes it's subtle and from within ourselves. While this is sometimes an unhealthy expression of competition, it can also reflect a desire to participate in God's mission, to meet the needs that are so obvious in our world: to repair the damage done to our environment, to ensure all people have adequate housing and enough food, to advance the civil rights of all people. These are big tasks that feel impossible to achieve, and on our own, they are impossible. The increased pressure of trying to make them happen by ourselves only adds to the avalanche of expectations upon us.

This is one reason our connections to a purpose greater than ourselves matters. If the mission is bigger than us, at some point we must also admit that we can't accomplish the mission on our own. That we're incapable of fixing everything might not be an easy thing to admit. But it can be liberating to admit that we are as God made us: finite. And finite creatures can't do infinite things, at least not alone. It is when we look to mission partners that we realize that even if we sometimes feel lonely or isolated by our callings, we're never truly alone in our vocations. We're connected with a boundless network of others living out their purpose and also working for the reconciliation of all things.

This reveals that we're not called to be everything for everyone. We can't possibly meet every need in all the universe. But we can meet the needs we encounter. There's a well-worn preaching image of a child walking along a shoreline one morning, finding it filled with beached sea stars abandoned by the shrinking tide. Knowing the sea stars will dry out and suffocate without the ocean's water, this kid rushes down the beach, throwing sea stars back into the ocean to ensure their survival. An adult, noticing the child's effort, comments that they couldn't possibly make a real difference, given the endless miles of seashore and countless sea stars. The child, ever hopeful and pragmatic, picks up yet another starfish, shows it to the adult, and says, "I made a difference for this one," before throwing it back into the water.

The vastness of the work led to the adult's despair, but the particular focus on what was possible in her realm helped the child focus on her particular vocation that day: saving the sea star she was able to put back in the water. That's the kind of awareness that helps us fulfill our specific purposes. Other partners could save other sea stars while she focused on this stretch of beach she walked, making a difference in her realm of influence. So, too, you can't solve global climate change on your own, nor can you ensure sustainable food sources for people throughout the earth or adequate education for all children. But like one former student of mine, you can choose to teach science in an underfunded school district and help kids learn about urban gardening and reusable energy resources in ways that affect their daily lives. Of course, this doesn't mean this now teacher is unconcerned with the systemic problems that ultimately need to be addressed. In fact, they also work with a local faith-based advocacy network to create policy change around education funding and energy sourcing. Rather than working in a silo, they work in partnership with other community leaders from other sectors.

Sometimes we're called to meet needs that aren't our primary gifts. For instance, my parents own a bit of property in rural Ohio, so as they age, I've taken more responsibility to care for that property. I'm no expert arborist, but I've learned to prune trees and split wood. I'm certainly no mason, but I've built my fair share of rock walls to prevent erosion. I'm no carpenter, but I've installed a few split rail fence posts. Just because I'm not a professional in these arenas doesn't mean I'm not called to fill those roles. Picasso doesn't need to paint the barn when others can accomplish that goal. In other words, we're not always the experts at our vocations; sometimes we're the ones available to do the meaningful, life-giving work that needs to be done.

Mission Statement

One of the practices I teach as a professor and consultant is to develop a personal mission statement that aligns with God's mission as my students and clients understand it. A mission statement should both describe your primary purpose and provide a constant catalyst to live that purpose.

True, mission statements don't solve everything. Not even a good mission statement can guarantee you'll act in accordance with your mission. It's up to you, once you've made it, to follow it as well.

For instance, my mission is to *empower others to clarify their identities and develop their vocations.* That's why I'm writing this book. If writing this weren't likely to help people distinguish between their identities and vocations, and if the practices I teach didn't help the people I've worked with to develop their vocations, then I wouldn't have spent countless hours researching, writing, and editing this text. I use the same kind of evaluation for my jobs as a pastor, professor, and center director. Whenever I'm asked to serve on a committee, teach a course, take a meeting, lead a project, or otherwise take on new work, I assess whether it fits with my personal mission statement. This isn't because my mission is so perfect. In fact, that's the third or fourth iteration of my mission statement since I entered campus ministry. But if I want my work to be meaningful and life-giving for others, then I first need to ensure that my personal mission aligns with what I understand to be God's universal mission, with the trajectory of the cosmos.

So how do you develop a mission statement?

First, keep it short and memorable, ideally under fifteen words. Some organizations I know don't have mission statements. They have mission paragraphs, even pages. I don't find that helpful. A good mission is one that you remember, that you can quickly repeat, that you don't need to look up because it's emblazoned in your memory.

Second, use verbs. Mission is what you do, after all, so when you create a mission statement, use language that indicates action. That's why my mission statement includes a primary action for me, to *empower,* as well as primary actions for the ways that I impact others, to *clarify* and to *develop*.

Third, be aware of how your mission relates to those you serve. A mission without an audience is not a vocation because it's not giving life to anyone outside yourself. You could be more specific about your audience than I am—after all, *others* is a broad category—but this generalization works given the other specifics of my mission that focus on certain populations.

Finally, a good mission statement will be specific enough to be actionable while general enough to be flexible. If your mission is so specific that it doesn't allow for creativity, then it is too narrowly defined. But if it's so generic that anyone could theoretically do that work, then it's not specifically your mission. For instance, my mission statement says nothing about young adults because I do this work with more than traditional undergraduate students. I guide graduate students, professional students, doctoral students, adult degree-completion students, and many others who aren't in the eighteen to thirty range. I also serve lots of ways in the church beyond young adult ministry, consulting with and leading worship among people of all ages.

Your sense of mission forms the connective tissue between the things you're called for (God's mission) and the thing you're called to (your vocations). Let's talk, then, about what you're called to and how you can identify those vocations.

The Specifics of Your Vocations

Each of us is called to particular work that is meaningful and life-giving for the world. Throughout the book, I've mentioned a number of possible vocations—in families, as citizens, in careers, through friendships, via service opportunities. Let's focus just a bit on each of these areas to understand how they can be vocations.

I'll start with families. While we're all born into a family of origin, not all of us stay with those families. Whether due to adoption, parental divorce, separation of certain members from the family for safety, or other reasons, sometimes we choose to develop another familial network, a family of choice. Yet no matter what our family structure, we each have roles in those families through which we provide meaningful work that gives life to others. As parents, we care for the bodily, social, educational, and relational needs of children. As siblings, we befriend, challenge, and support one another. Extended family members play numerous roles as coaches, mentors, teachers, cheerleaders, guides, counselors, and more. We do much meaningful work in our family, from the mundane to the extraordinary, that gives life to others.

So, too, citizens are called to act in ways that are meaningful and life-giving to the country (and for people of every nation). In the United States, our vocation includes voluntary participation in the voting process and obligated service when called for jury duty. Countries such as Brazil, Israel, Nigeria, and South Korea require temporary military service as a part of citizenship. In France, a relatively new mandate requires all citizens to spend a month of their sixteenth year learning service skills, and youth are encouraged to volunteer for a longer period after the obligation is complete. In these and myriad other ways, citizens provide meaningful work that gives life to others in their countries.

Careers are those things most often identified as vocations, in no small part because we sometimes call career centers "vocational schools." Yet vocations are not limited to jobs. Some people don't practice typical professions or trades, especially with the rise of the gig economy. Our vocational careers are the ways we earn a livelihood. For a fortunate sector, this livelihood includes a salary and benefits. For some, this includes hourly work, temp work, consulting work, and other temporary roles. Others earn a living through bartering rather than participating in a cash economy. Still others don't have careers at all, whether because they've never started that work, have been forced out of an occupation, are unable to hold a typical job for various reasons, or have chosen to stop work. That's yet another reason why we can't collapse vocation narrowly into the concept of career. Just because you don't have a job that pays doesn't mean you don't have a call of significance. You do as a family member, citizen, and in other arenas.

One of those vital vocations is that of friendship. To befriend someone is a choice to invest in someone to whom you're not obligated by law or family ties. Friendships develop in many aspects of life—school, work, activities like music or athletics—so friends share interests, experiences, or purposes that are distinct from those of family. The drive to friendship transcends basic biology. Friendship isn't about ensuring our lineage or passing on our DNA. There's something beyond physiology, something downright spiritual, about friendships that makes the world a better place not just for us but for others.

We can even perform meaningful, life-giving work on behalf of those we don't naturally care about, for those we're not inclined to befriend, through service to humankind and to the wider world. While selflessness is an element of all our vocations, I use *service* here for the work we freely offer on behalf of those to whom we're not obliged as family, friends, coworkers, or the like. To pick up garbage from your neighborhood and to reduce your carbon footprint by using fewer fossil fuels are both forms of service. To feed those who are hungry right now and to organize political and social capital to eradicate food insecurity are both acts of service. Every form of service affirms others' identities and vocations. Habits of service are pregnant with meaning and bestow life far beyond our most proximate communities.

What Vocation Is Not

We are called to family, to citizenship, to career, to friendship, to service, and other vocations, though these are the most common—and each is holy. But not all labor is vocation. If the work isn't meaningful or life-giving, it's not vocation. Now, this isn't a reason to write off dull, mentally taxing, or physically demanding work. Sometimes, difficult work is still meaningful work, like changing a baby's diapers is meaningful to their health. Yet some use work in oppressive ways that remove all meaning. Slavery, for instance, is not a vocation, not for those enslaved or their so-called masters (read: tyrants). Forced labor is not holy work but the oppressive result of greed and prejudice.

Other kinds of activities are not sinful but are also not vocations. For instance, my wife and I recently sold our first house in Columbus, Ohio, which in just over three years accrued over 30 percent in value. Just because that transaction produced a profit doesn't mean selling it was a vocation—meaningful, life-giving work—for us. However, real estate agents, inspectors, title agents, and others did practice their vocations in the sale of our home.

Still other kinds of work aren't meaningful or life-giving. I think of general busywork here—not the kind of administrative work that is the vocation of office managers and administrative assistants, who empower others to do different work well, but the kind of tasks that are sometimes assigned simply to keep an employee (or a child) busy. The television series *Lost* once depicted this with perfection. I'd give you a spoiler warning, but since the show aired from 2004 to 2010, you've had your chance. In *Lost*, a plane crash strands passengers on an island they soon discover is abnormal in a number of ways. One early discovery is evidence of supernatural forces at play on the island, and another is that there's apparently a history of human habitation and experimentation. One such research site includes instructions to record observations and send notebooks full of that data through pneumatic tubes to an unknown headquarters for uncertain reasons. Some characters do so diligently. In later episodes, a traveling group happens upon a miniature mountain of capsules, seemingly thousands of notebooks full of information that was sent not to the nonexistent HQ but to nowhere. That was work for researchers and recorders alike, but it was meaningless, sapping life from them and dumping it in an open grave of clear plastic and college-ruled sheets.

Now, in your life, no one is likely to ask you to record the behaviors of your colleagues and share the information with an unknown research group. But how many pointless meetings have you attended that should have been an email? What about the sailor who is asked to scrub a deck that's just been cleaned by another? What about reorganizing storage closets that are already usefully organized? Sometimes, we're asked to do work, by others or ourselves, that doesn't serve a purpose beyond itself. That's not vocation.

Your specific work, in the various vocations you encounter, has connections to the transcendent, but it is not your job to do everything. Nor are you obligated to do work that doesn't have clear meaning to you or to others. In that sweet spot on the spectrum, somewhere between the poles of doing nothing worthwhile and taking responsibility for the whole universe, you will find specific purposes with cosmic significance.

Specific Vocations for a Transcendent Mission

You're called to work that is meaningful for you and life-giving for the world. This includes work in many arenas, but they're more than just jobs, or ways to make money, or burdens of obligation. They're stations in life that fulfill holy purpose for you and for others. This is true of your family life, of your career, of your citizenship, and more. It's not work you're forced to do, nor is it effortless, but it is work you choose to do because it is work worth the effort—that worth seen through the meaning made manifest and the life that appears through the work.

With all this in mind, then, you might wonder how you know specifically which career you're called to, or how you want to support your family, or what kind of citizen you want to be. That questioning is natural, and in fact, it's often the most difficult part of vocation. A clear sense of what you're called to in all the potential realms of vocation is not easy to come by, especially with so many voices competing for your attention. So how do you get clarity? That's where we turn now, to equip you with tools to identify the specific ways you're called to meaningful, life-giving work in the world.

Part 2

4D Formation

Now we turn from conversation about concepts to a focus on practices. In the previous chapters, I've described what vocation is and the various ways we can experience callings to our vocations. We experience callings as whole people. We experience callings through our communities. We experience callings for a transcendent purpose beyond ourselves. And we experience callings to live out that transcendent purpose in specific ways.

It's that last experience of calling that confounds so many people. How do we choose the vocations through which we will find meaningful and life-giving work for the world? How might we move from the *theory* of vocation to the *practice* of our vocations? This section offers a process I call 4D Formation. The four Ds are *discovery*, *discernment*, *development*, and *decision*.

In the introduction, I talked about these four Ds as dimensions of vocational exploration because, that's right, the journey of vocational exploration includes a sense of time travel. When we activate our vocations, our God-given callings reflect a holy eternity here in real time. By living our sacred purposes, we reveal a piece of heaven on earth. Vocational exploration is the interwoven process of discovery, discernment, development, and decision that guides us into the vocations of our lives. Activating our vocations connects us with eternal purpose, participating in heaven on earth.

Just because I talk about discovery, discernment, development, and decision in that order doesn't mean the process of identifying our vocations is linear. We can't simply tidy up our vocations—though trust me, I wish we could apply Marie Kondo's guidance in this way. Instead, the process is much more like the way we live every day. We simultaneously discover, discern, develop, and decide. The process is a part of life's journey, where every discovery leads to decision, every development leads to discernment. It's not linear, but neither is life.

So if you are looking for an instruction booklet with a detailed map from points A to Z, unfortunately, this isn't it. To follow the metaphor we've been using so far, 4D Formation is a legend for reading the maps of vocational exploration that others give to us and for interpreting the maps we create along the way. Discovery, discernment, development, and decision help orient us on the journey, identify where we are, and point us toward where we want to be. These help us read the information we encounter in our environment and within ourselves. With the compass of faith, the maps we develop, and the mission we identify, 4D Formation helps us first set goals and then navigate our journeys.

Knowing that the process isn't linear, we still must start somewhere. Let's begin with discovery, because with new knowledge comes a new sense of what is possible for our vocations.

Chapter 6

Discovering What's Possible

Think of discovery as a catalyst for a chemical change. Catalysts either start a chemical reaction or speed up one already in progress. For instance, if you leave soda unsealed, you know that it will slowly release all the carbonation, leaving you a very flat, and therefore very disappointing, drink. If you drop a mint in a two-liter bottle of soda when you first unseal it, the combination of chemicals in the candy and the soda speeds up the release of gasses, leading to a massive explosion of fizzy pop. (Yes, I use *soda* and *pop* interchangeably after growing up in the Midwest but spending nearly a decade in the South. But I digress.) The point is, the reaction happens slowly without the catalyst, but adding the candy to the liquid really kicks it into high gear.

Discovery, intentional and otherwise, is that catalyst for vocational exploration. We spend much of our lives thinking about the work that we do, but we're not always intentional about that thought process. Sometimes we're complacent about the status quo, not thinking about how we can make meaningful, life-giving contributions to our neighbors and just going through the motions of life. Sometimes we're self-absorbed, concerned more with increasing wealth or reducing effort than with how we'll make a positive impact on the world around us. Like a soda left open on the counter, we may slowly lose the bubbly energy created by possible vocations rather than direct it toward something of significance.

Discovery is the catalyst that leads to explosive possibilities in your vocational journey. Rather than allowing the energy to slowly dissipate, discovery redirects it toward many possibilities, perhaps even excitement. After all, it's impossible to know what vocational options are available to you without first discovering those options exist. Yet discovery doesn't cease. This is where the candy-and-pop metaphor falls apart, because after the initial burst that follows the catalyst, the soda is all gone, with the gases released into the air and sticky-sweet liquid strewn on the ground. Discovery is the kind of catalyst that can keep the reaction going long term, like uranium in a nuclear reactor, constantly creating energy with great potential. So, too, vocational discoveries continue to lead to new opportunities throughout life. For instance, after I became a pastor, I discovered the possibility of becoming a professor and an author, things that seemed impossible years ago. Vocational opportunities can appear at seemingly every turn, especially if you're attentive to the world in which you live.

In 4D Formation, discovery is an intentional exercise. Of course, some discoveries happen by accident. After all, we're not the only ones in control of what we discover. Other people share knowledge with us. We run into so much information on our journeys, from fellow journeyers to obstacles, geography to opportunities. To explore our vocations is to adopt a deliberate disposition that welcomes new possibilities. Without discovery, our vocational possibilities are limited by the worldviews we acquire from our narrow fields of vision. While others will certainly introduce new opportunities to us, those opportunities may not align with our values, our missions, or our skills. Further, while every person bears God's image, not everyone bears our best interest in mind. We must be diligent in discovery, always open to learn from the new information we encounter.

That's why I constantly say that vocation requires exploration. To explore, you must make a conscious effort to find new things, to engage in new experiences, to learn new information. You don't accidentally become an explorer; you choose to explore. Explorers are active seekers. Explorers intend to discover new things and consider how to incorporate those discoveries in their lives, even if they challenge them or change their purpose.

It's essential for us as vocational explorers to envision most anything as possible, at least at first. Eventually, through discernment and development, the options will decrease as values, skills, and passions shape the decisions we make. The list of possibilities will quickly become more manageable with honest assessments of our desires and experiences. But at first, an open mind allows us to see something of worth in many of the options we discover. We too often ignore vocational discoveries because they seem too difficult to attain, or too far beyond our skill sets, or simply too alien to our experiences. Eventually, you will determine whether something's truly your call, but to do so faithfully, you must entertain the possibility that it *could* be your call. To deny a possibility without consideration ignores the transcendent nature of call and the communal influence on your sense of purpose. Such sincere reflection can also strengthen your convictions in your vocations as you claim them, for you know you've truly explored a variety of holy possibilities.

Before we examine the powerful potential for discovery on your vocational journey, though, let's consider some of the dangers.

Dangers of Discovery

Recently, in a conversation with a few students of mine, we talked about discovery and the terrible legacy of colonialism. European colonizers left their shores with a simple, devastating presumption: if they discovered something—a resource, a piece of land, even a people—it belonged to them (or to the sponsor who funded their explorations). Though Indigenous populations lived in and cared for the lands from Asia to Africa to the Americas, Europeans decided that their discovery entitled them to claim these continents and their assets as their own. They acted as though these lands, inhabited and cared for by People of Color for millennia, now belonged to white colonizers simply because they planted a flag into the soil they'd just discovered. The sins of selfishness, racism, and Eurocentrism reveal the danger of assuming that discovery determines ownership. Discovery of something does not entitle us to possession. It should increase our awareness of what exists and open us to the potential of new possibilities, but just because we discover something doesn't mean it belongs to us. That's why discovery is a part of the process rather than the sum of vocational exploration.

Natural resources are certainly different from vocational possibilities. Even so, not every vocation you discover belongs to you. To claim a vocation that isn't yours is harmful not only for you but for others. It might put you in work situations that don't have meaning because they don't align with your values. Or it might place you in work that you're not prepared or skilled for, so rather than being life-giving, the work becomes life-sapping, if not life-threatening. (That's me in a carpenter shop.) So it's OK for you to spend time with parents of children without feeling called to be a parent yourself. It's fine to know partners in a marriage and not be called to become a spouse yourself. Discovery opens the world of vocations to us. Discovering what's possible shows us the values in those vocations as someone inhabits them. But it doesn't mean we must inhabit each of them.

Relatedly, just because we discover something doesn't mean others haven't discovered it before. To act as though we're the first to inhabit an ancient call lacks a necessary humility. Many others have walked the journey of vocational exploration and experienced what we've just discovered. Some of them have created maps we can consider. We should invite elders to share wisdom and mentors to coach us in our paths to vocational clarity. We need to maintain a willingness to hear from others about the history of what we've discovered and the meaning or significance it has for them. Imagine how differently European exploration would have been carried out if travelers had approached new wonders with humility and how different our present world would be as a result of that humility.

Humility in the journey keeps us from making rash choices. For instance, one of the things you learn when hiking in a new place is that just because you discover a path doesn't mean it is yours to take. When I was a college student, some peers and I spent spring break hiking in the Gila National Forest in New Mexico, a beautiful preserve with a river at the bottom of a thousand-foot canyon and a plateau of desert and scrub forest atop the canyon. One day, a small group of us decided to hike up the canyon and then a nearby mountain, which we did in short order. After taking in the panoramic view of the vast New Mexico wilderness, we descended to the plateau, with the canyon still far below, only to find fresh mountain lion tracks and scat (polite trail language for poop) in the middle of the path. To avoid the predator's interest, we left our path and walked in the opposite direction from the big cat's prints, certain we could circle around to find the path again.

Except, we lost the trail.

So for the next four hours, we wandered the plateau, finding our way to the canyon rim but unable to find the path that led down into the canyon and back to our base camp on the river. Not planning to be gone for that long, we hadn't rationed our water. We found ourselves thirsty, delirious, and hell-bent on finding a way back to our water source and base camp, not to mention as far as possible from our new feline friend. So as soon as I found what looked like a way to climb down the canyon, I began to take it even though it clearly wasn't the path that we'd taken to the top. To be abundantly clear, this was not a hiking trail. It was a series of ledges that would require free-climbing at various points. Further, we could only see a portion of the descent. In theory, the path might have led to the river, but it was neither safe nor smart to take it. In my pride, I sought a path that wasn't ours to take. Fortunately, another member of the group reminded us that if we kept walking along the ledge in the direction from which we had come, we would intersect the trail and find a safe, assured descent back to the rest of our group. That's just what we did. Sometimes, discovery shows us what is possible for others but not for ourselves, at least not without better tools or more knowledge.

But just because you discover something doesn't mean that the discovery is without flaw. For instance, the map you have in mind when you picture the world is almost certainly inaccurate. The maps mostly commonly used for centuries, the ones you most likely discovered in elementary geography, have been based on the Mercator projection, a map developed by Flemish geographer and cartographer

Gerardus Mercator in 1569. It's even the basis of the map you see when you zoom out for a worldwide view on your smartphone's map applications. This map, because it presents a globe on a flat sheet, significantly inflates the size of land masses that are farther from the equator, including northern Asia, Europe, and North America, which distorts the relative size of Africa and other equatorial land masses. In reality, you could fit the entire landmass of the United States, Russia, and Greenland inside of Africa and still have plenty of room to spare, but the Mercator projection makes that seem impossible.

Another example: for most of my first twenty years of life, I assumed Jesus was white because, well, literally every picture I saw of Jesus depicted him as some kind of Swiss ski instructor who just got off alpine slopes. More than once I imagined this Christ was on his way to a hot tub and hot chocolate after cutting some fresh powder. Warner Sallman's famous painting of Jesus, which has hung in countless church basements and lounges, has fixed this idea into many North American minds. The image was nearly sealed for me by Mel Gibson's casting of Jim Caviezel as Jesus in *The Passion of the Christ*, which I saw on what had to be the strangest youth group outing I've ever been on. Of course, though, Jesus was a Semitic Jew. He had brown skin, with ancestral ties to Canaan as well as North Africa, Arabia, and Persia. My first encounter with a depiction of Jesus as a Semite was in 2001, when I saw a forensic anthropologist's reconstruction of the face of a first-century Israeli skeleton.[1] This Jesus was much shorter than most images I'd seen, with much darker, shorter hair; bronze-brown skin; and wouldn't you know it, none of the abdominal definition that many crucifixes give to white Jesus. Jesus did not, in all likelihood, have a six-pack. I had to discover images of Jesus from outside my family of faith to realize that he wasn't a white dude.

Just because you discover something doesn't mean it's new for everyone, and it certainly doesn't mean you own it now that you've discovered it. Just because you find a path doesn't mean it's yours to take. Just because something you discover seems right, don't immediately trust that the depiction matches reality. Be aware of these dangers, but don't let them stop you from experiencing the powerful potential for discovery to activate your vocational journey.

A Legendary Search Process

When we look at a map, we see lines, dots, dashes, and other symbols of various colors—markings we must interpret. We won't necessarily comprehend all the information the map contains, even if we recognize some general features. That's where the importance of a legend comes in.

Remember that a legend is what unlocks the symbols on the map. Another word for a *legend* is a *key*, because it opens the door to understanding the map. On a good map, all of the symbols are explained, so we can interpret objects, colors, shapes, and various types of lines. Understanding the legend is a necessary step to reading the map and, in turn, navigating the environments we're exploring so we can more accurately interpret the landmarks we encounter on our journey.

Remember that the map for our vocations isn't made of folded paper, nor is it a digital application. It is the collection of stories and experiences we gather from others and from ourselves as we consider life's purpose. Unfortunately, life doesn't come with a single legend that enables us to accurately interpret every environment we enter. There's no master key to unlock all the universe's wisdom. But that doesn't mean we have no tools to illuminate our journey. 4D Formation acts as a legend to help you make sense of this map and navigate your paths. As you explore your vocation, pay close attention to the things that have helped you navigate the landscape so far. Your values are a part of the legend, pointing to what is truly meaningful. Your faith is a part of the legend, pointing toward true north. Your experience is a part of the legend, identifying the paths you've crossed before and the terrain you've already navigated. In other words, the legend for your vocational exploration helps you interpret your lived experience.

The people we encounter, our communities, also help make sense of the map. As I said in chapter 4, each community has been something of a constellation, a sign in the sky that orients me as I explore my vocation. No community is the same, as is no grouping of stars. Each takes on a different shape and personality, whether a Taurus bull or a Gemini twin or an Orion hunter. And each tells me something about the journey, where I am in relation to my past and my future.

Part of discovery is navigating your path with a focus on both the legend and the stars. Be mindful of the experience you bring and the landscape you encounter, interpreting it in light of what you know. At the same time, attend to the stars—the communities in your life that offer other perspectives, that share other wisdom. As you look to your legend and to the stars who help shape it, you can see how your journey intersects with the journeys of others and how your legend is enlightened by the wisdom of others. Such a constellation can be a powerful key to unlocking your vocations. Using this legend to help guide your next steps can make this journey, well, legendary.

Discovery Is Empowerment

As you undertake this journey of vocational exploration, you enter a realm pregnant with power. People disagree about the origins of the phrase "Knowledge is power." Some argue that Sir Francis Bacon coined the phrase, others Thomas Hobbes. But I first encountered it in *Schoolhouse Rock!*, that great source of wisdom that gathered and educated many children in the 1990s. This cartoon made learning fun through short musical numbers like "I'm Just a Bill," which taught kids about the US legislative process, and "Conjunction Junction," which helped children understand the function of conjunctions in language. Both the theme song and sign-off included the line "Knowledge is power." This phrase became an inspiration for many artists, from meme makers across the internet to Seth MacFarlane, creator of the television series *Family Guy*. In the same era, *G.I. Joe* cartoons ended with public service announcements about everything from not leaving the water running to avoiding downed powerlines, and each would end with "Knowing is half the battle," which became another ubiquitous meme and pop-culture reference in later shows like *Community*. What these shows tried to instill in children is the principle that learning is a source of power in times of war and peace. While internet and sitcom references don't prove that this goal was reached, they show, at least, a lasting impact of the lesson.

That's what discovery is ultimately about: knowledge. Discovery empowers us with knowledge of what is possible, for us and for others. To know what is possible frees us to have a vision beyond what already is right now. There's a significant difference between what options exist and the vocations we inhabit, both now and in the future. However, discovery leads to more knowledge, and more knowledge expands the range of vocations for us to consider.

Faithful and fruitful discovery relies on the tools I've spoken of throughout the book: making a map, learning a legend, using a compass. I mean *faithful* not as a predetermined outcome but instead as formed by the faith or worldview you call your own and by the identity that reflects your sacred worth. Your faithful discovery, while sharing significant overlap with that of others, will ultimately look different from theirs because your journey is uniquely yours. It's not disconnected from others or from your traditions, for you can learn from the maps that have been made before, and the compass of faith keeps you grounded as you pursue the possible. It's your use of a legend, though, that helps you read the signs of the times.

When I learned that Jesus wasn't white, that discovery was powerful. It empowered me with a different picture in my mind of what God looks like in the flesh. It gave me the ability to see Jesus more authentically as a historical Palestinian figure and to see how other cultures might interpret Jesus with different ethnic features. It empowered me to see the ways that whiteness, both intentionally and accidentally, takes up space from People of Color. It empowered me to confront my own biases as a white person raised in a predominantly white town in rural Ohio. Similarly, when I learned that the map of the world in my head was distorted, that knowledge empowered me to reconsider the data I considered absolutely true, not only about geography, but about, well, everything, including faith. Because something I took to be absolute was, in fact, only true from a certain position, I began to reassess other things I thought were certain and ask how different perspectives might shape the subject. I learned those things from members of my community, who helped me redraw my map in more accurate ways.

Discovery gives us the power to see truth from other perspectives, seeing the different ways truth is shown through the prisms in our lives. With that new information, we challenge the notions others have given us. Engaging with others, who see prisms and the light cast through them at different angles, helps us and others comprehend more fully the substance of our discoveries. Discovery opens us to new possibilities beyond our origins and new opportunities beyond our preconceptions.

That kind of discovery is different from that of colonial explorers. Rather than seeking to rule over what is discovered, we can undertake discovery as modeled by the leaders of an ancient Indian religion, Jain Dharma, sometimes called Jainism in the West. The spiritual teachers of Jain Dharma are known as *tirthankaras*, literally, "ford makers." These leaders are known for sixteen commitments, one of which is relentlessly seeking knowledge. What's fascinating about *tirthankaras* is that rather than earning a degree or gaining social status, they use the spiritual knowledge gained to help others experience liberation. They build bridges to help people span the gap from this existence to the next, to ford the river into nirvana (which they also call *moksha*). They are discoverers who help others discover what is possible.

The witness of their names, ford makers, struck me. As Jains understand these ford makers, they've discovered the absolute truth, eternal personal meaning and unending life, and yet rather than become self-absorbed, they instead commit to empowering others to make that discovery as well. Discovery, in this view, isn't meant to be hoarded; it's meant to be shared.

Understanding discovery in this way, as a kind of humble sharing, benefits from intentional learning, one with your vocation in mind and one that seeks both meaning for yourself and abundant life for others. Let me share a few practices that I've seen prove powerfully useful for people exploring their vocational possibilities.

Discovery Practices

While any number of practices can foster discovery, one that I've found almost universally helpful is mindfulness. Mindfulness is not the same thing as meditation, though they're often conflated. Meditation and prayer practices often include kinds of mindfulness, but not necessarily. Similarly, mindfulness as a practice can exist apart from meditation. So what is mindfulness and how can it help you discover what's possible for your purpose?

Mindfulness is the practice of intentional awareness, active attentiveness to things that we often take for granted. We might focus on our bodies—our heartbeat or our breath or the subtle feelings of tension in our muscles. We might notice the sounds of unseen birds in nearby trees or the weariness in the eyes of a fellow bus passenger. We might notice our environment—the low hum of the electricity that powers the lights in your home, the nuance in coloration between grass blades, or the slight variation in the woodgrain of the table as you run your hand over it. To be mindful is to become intentionally aware of ourselves, others, and our environment. This intentional awareness also includes things in our minds that we may try to suppress. Often, when one of my Buddhist colleagues begins a mindfulness exercise, she encourages us to become aware of not only the environment around us but the thoughts within us. Rather than judge ourselves or see these thoughts as distractions, she reminds us to acknowledge them as a part of our experience and then to set them aside so we might deepen the practice at hand.

Mindfulness enables us to become more aware of our environment, of ourselves, and of the relationship between ourselves and our environment. It even helps us understand our relationship with ourselves. That's how mindfulness can help us discover possible vocations. Rather than hurtle through the universe accidentally, mindfulness increases our awareness of where we are and empowers us with the capacity to evaluate our present. Then if we're not satisfied with our present, we can make changes to our path to pursue new goals.

Researchers have identified two relevant discovery practices that support student success: research and experiments.[2] We research things all the time, often without thinking about what we're doing. We research the ingredients in and nutritional quality of our food. We research the fit of our clothing. We research the assisted living facilities where aging family members might live by asking others about their experiences. The same kind of awareness that helps you be mindful of what your breath feels like or the unique texture of different kinds of apples can be used to undergird purposeful practices of vocational discovery. To be sure, this is more than reading news headlines and social media posts and saying, "I'm doing my own research." To research possible vocations, you can read memoirs or watch documentaries about people with various backgrounds. Study job descriptions to see what's included in the base expectations. Interview, even informally, people whose lives you find inspiring. Job shadowing can be a powerful introduction to a career. Babysitting can help you understand what it's like to be responsible for a child before you choose parenthood. Using free time to try new things, from kayaking in a local park to visiting a museum to attending a dance class, can reveal skills, passions, growing edges, and obstacles to various vocations. The information you glean through such research can help you become more aware of both what's possible and what the possibilities entail.

Once you've learned something from these initial introductions, you can take part in experiments or immersions for deeper discoveries. If during a job shadow you discover an interest in dentistry, an internship in a dental office can help you better understand what the opportunity might be like. If you find interest in law, assisting in a legal office or pro bono clinic can deepen your awareness of both the practice and the impact lawyers can make. If you fall in love with nature during leisure hikes or camping trips, a part-time job in a local state or national park can broaden your perspective on the kinds of work available in the field.

All of these experiences entail calculated risk. Such risks are calculated because we intend to take them with the potential costs and benefits in mind. Remember my desire to make a path down the cliffs of a canyon? That was *not* a calculated risk. I lacked an awareness of my abilities and the path ahead. Calculated risks require investing time in research, money in resources, and effort in experiments, and even our own vulnerabilities in discovering new information that might challenge our sense of self and clarity of purpose. Make no mistake: these are risks. You might discover you are not ready, that you do not possess the necessary financial or relational resources, even that something you loved is not, in fact, a viable vocation for you. This is where discovery turns to discernment, another part of 4D Formation, which I'll address in the next chapter.

But you, dear one, are worth the risk. Your vocation is worth the risk of vulnerability. These practices—mindfulness, research, and experimentation—are just a few ways that you can participate in your vocational discovery. I've seen students entirely uninterested in pastoral work catch fire for ministry after one pastoral immersion. I've seen students apparently committed to a career in accounting discover a passion for visual arts through an elective course. An openness to possibilities invites you to discover the surprising potential vocations that are available for you.

Mentors to Guide the Way

One last key to discovery that's essential to both identity formation and vocational exploration is a mentor—or better yet, multiple mentors—to guide the way. Mentors, members of the communities through which we're called, are part spiritual advisor, part trail guide, and part coach. Ideally, mentors will pray for you and keep you connected to the transcendent purpose to which you've aligned your life. Seek mentors who've walked similar journeys or blazed comparable trails. Look for mentors who will cheer you on, correct your wrongs, affirm your rights, and stick with you. Mentors help remind you, perhaps more than any other person, that you're not alone on this journey of vocational exploration and that the discoveries you make offer possibilities worth pursuing.

Good practices for discovery are even better when practiced alongside someone who has your best intentions at heart. I'm fortunate that many mentors chose to walk my journey with me. Some focused my attention on my environment, helping me become more mindful. Some discussed my research with me and pointed me toward new resources for study. Some invited me to shadow them on a job or complete an internship to experience vocational possibilities firsthand. Some pushed me to my growing edges so I could learn I was capable of more than I thought was possible.

I encourage you to choose your mentors wisely. Simply because someone is good at other vocations doesn't mean they'll be a good mentor for you, because, perhaps obviously, mentorship is a vocation too! Plenty of good cooks can't teach people to cook. Plenty of good parents can't empower people to care for children. Part of finding a mentor is about finding someone who is not only good at what they do but capable of helping others become good at it too.

More important, though, is the fact that just because someone is capable of teaching doesn't mean they're a good fit for you. Finding a fit between mentor and mentee personalities—both in their similarities and in their differences—is often a huge benefit for mentoring relationships. Mentoring is both a practical vocation and a spiritual practice. It is work that brings the meaning in our lives and others' lives together. It also provides an opportunity for a healthy intimacy that acknowledges a connection beyond ourselves, a note of the transcendence of spirituality. Like the ford makers of Jain Dharma, mentors can help us bridge from our present place and into the space where God is calling us.

Turning to Discernment

Discovery can be both exhilarating and daunting. Even so, throughout that spectrum, discovery is vital to an invigorated process of vocational exploration. Without discovery, you'd never know what vocational options exist. Once you've identified a wide array of options, you might begin to ask, "What do I do with all this information?" Fortunately, another disposition in 4D Formation helps one assess the value, relevancy, and fit of all these discoveries. Let's shift our lens to that question and focus on discernment.

Chapter 7

Demystifying Discernment

Who among us hasn't felt overwhelmed? Sometimes the responsibilities that face us weigh heavily on our shoulders. At other times, the challenges caused by limitations in ourselves or others engulf us. A more recent source of anxiety in twenty-first-century North America is the vast array of options available to us. Should we choose to play an instrument, learn a sport, or take up a hobby, few of us can easily choose one from among the mountain of possibilities. Not only do grocery stores offer myriad choices, but countless restaurants serve nearly any cuisine at varied price points. Entertainment choices include nearly endless music, sports, television series, and movies, which you can enjoy live, recorded, or streamed.

So of course, when it comes to choices like what college you might attend or how to choose a romantic partner or what career you might consider, you carry not only the import of those decisions but the burden of more options than you can possibly conceive of into the decision-making process itself. How can you feel confident with your vocational decisions when the number of options seems so intimidating? You discern.

Discernment is another one of those words that's frequently used in colleges and religious communities without a clear, common definition. Sometimes we're told to do the work of discernment but not shown how to discern. At other times, especially in church communities, leaders tell people to listen for God's voice or seek God's plan. Mysterious, indeed—and not terribly helpful without clear practices of discernment.

The goal here isn't to remove God from the discernment process; it's to clarify discernment so we can engage the sacred more clearly and comprehend that presence more palpably. Since spirituality is involved, there's always some transcendent mystery. After all, as one prophet wrote, God's ways are not our ways (Isa 55:8). Yet the source of our callings invites us to learn the ways of sacred worth, to inhabit our identities as holy image bearers, to embody holy presence throughout our lives. To clarify, discernment is one way for us to increase our communion with the divine.

To discern is to evaluate and rank possibilities. Discernment might involve prioritizing discoveries you've made throughout your life. As you explore your vocation, however, discernment especially relates to your identity as one of sacred worth and to your role in God's mission. It also takes into account your skills and limitations as well as your passions and the needs you most care about in the world.

Who's Calling Whom?

You might remember from chapter 1 that another common word for vocation is *calling*, since the root word of *vocation* means "to call." You might hear people talk about feeling "called" to something or say they have found their "calling." You are called to meaningful, life-giving work for the world. But by whom? Who is calling?

My tradition, Lutheranism, speaks about an internal and external call. One way we determine priorities is by noticing if the internal call matches the external call. This might sound like strangely technical insider language, but let me explain.

The internal call is that personal sense of purpose, passion, or meaning you find in a particular kind of work. If you feel compelled to make a difference in the world through coaching youth sports or writing inspiring music, your feeling of purpose or desire to work in these particular ways is an internal call.

The external call comes from outside yourself, a beckoning from others to a particular kind of work. When a local nonprofit asks you to help serve food to alleviate hunger or to advocate for laws that will decrease food insecurity, their request is an external call. When I tell my students that they're effective leaders and encourage them to consider running for the executive board to help our campus ministry thrive, that's an external call. When others see capacities or potentials in you and affirm your use of them in ways that give life to others, that's an external call.

The concept of external call takes on even more meaning if we keep in mind the truth that everyone bears God's image in some way. The sacred can speak to us through the words of not just prophets or scriptures but our neighbors and friends. When you experience an external call, it's not just a person speaking on their own but a chorus of human and divine voices together calling you toward your vocations.

One way to know that you're called to something is that the internal and external calls match. If there's synergy between your passions and the affirmations you receive from your community, it's likely you are being called. If there's a lack of alignment between your internal and external call, that's not the last word, but it certainly means there's more discernment needed. For instance, if you feel an internal call to be a cook but find few people willing to eat the food you prepare, much less buy it, then there's more discernment to be done. Perhaps you need to find a different audience for your cooking. Perhaps you need to take cooking classes. Perhaps you need to source different ingredients. Perhaps you need to explore other vocations.

Legends and Stars Again

We've already seen that legends are vital parts of interpreting your journey, but here we see why they're so important. You as an explorer decide if you're headed to the mountains or the beach, to the city or the country, and whether you'll take the main roads or the byways. Legends reveal the meaning of symbols on the map—red stars for capitals, blue lines for waterways, green areas for protected natural land. A legend doesn't describe the inherent value of any feature, but it does provide information about factors that may play a major part in your journey. It's up to you to decide what's important about that information and how it relates to your path—which route you want to take, where you want to stop, and what resources you need to sustain yourself as you explore. Those indications will have different values for different journeys. For instance, if you're in a Fiat 500, you're likely to prefer country roads to the railroad. If you're hiking, you're probably looking for footpaths rather than the interstate. This likely feels obvious, but it reveals the value of a legend.

While there's no official map for vocational exploration, you can create one based on the landscapes, routes, and landmarks that you or others have discovered. You can use 4D Formation as a legend for your map—which includes mentors and communities, your religious or spiritual tradition along with other identity markers—and undertake the journey with the practices I describe in what follows. With the help of your legend, the map can help you clarify how important any of the aspects are to given portions of your journey. Your family of origin will not always be the most important aspect. Nor will your skills or experiences. But they, along with a host of other factors, each contribute to the landscape of your life. Knowing that they're there and how to identify them can make your journey to purpose more clear.

Sometimes, though, fog hides the landmarks. Erosion changes the river's path. The tides shift the shoreline. Or you're in uncharted territory. What do you do when the legends you've created don't describe the experiences of your world? You can look to the stars or the compass. Sometimes, even the faintest twinkling of a familiar star can provide a needed course correction. Some stars are theological, like my tradition's affirmation of the world's goodness and God's grace, the commitments we hold because God chose to both create the earth and then take on human form in Jesus. What makes these stars more significant than landmarks is that religious rituals often imbue an incredible depth of meaning for central concepts that remain even after other aspects of the religion seem to disappear. In other words, some people still value rituals from their childhood church, synagogue, mosque, or temple even after they've left that faith tradition behind. Think, for instance, of how the practice of confession and forgiveness can establish the importance of honesty and grace in people who no longer identify as Christian—and even some who critique the church for not practicing what the rituals preach! Still other stars are literary, like Rumi's poetry and the Rev. Dr. Martin Luther King Jr.'s "Letter from Birmingham Jail." Some stars are visual, like He Qi's biblical paintings and the mandalas of many Asian religious traditions. These things communicate truth in ways that guide my life, even and perhaps especially amid changing landscapes.

Remember also that your spiritual tradition or worldview can provide a compass to orient your life. More than the individual beliefs or practices, which can act as guiding stars, the whole of the tradition can provide a magnetic force to orient your life throughout many possible journeys. Identifying true north can be a lifesaver when the fog covers even the stars. When we can't see those constants, we can feel increasingly isolated, even though we trust they remain there. Just as you use a compass to guide your steps when you can't trust the landscape or see the sky, your faith can direct your choices when all other resources seem out of reach.

As you explore your vocation, it's important to create a map so you can navigate the journey of your calling. It's also important to realize that landscapes can change. Glaciers carve great lakes, and shifting tectonic plates create high mountains and deep trenches. The world in which you're called to work is constantly shifting in vast and small ways. So your map and the legends you make should also identify the stars that can guide you even when the shifting sands remake your paths and the true north that orients you even when the stars don't seem to shine.

Weighing Your Options for Abundant Life

Options don't have to be scary. That observation begins with the previous chapter's clarification that not everything you discover belongs to you. This is certainly true with foods, colleges, and entertainment and also with life partners, careers, and even voting options. It's also true with vocation. Just because you come across a path doesn't mean it is your path to take.

One way to think about paths is to consider the concept of sin. Sadly, in the Christian tradition, sin has become a kind of billy club in the hand of purity culture, one that leads to shame rather than liberation, to judgment rather than fulfillment. Theology that operates as a weapon of oppression rather than as a tool of liberation is dangerous and, in the most fundamental use of the term, anti-Christ. I confess that we've done that and, further, that I've done that both before and after my ordination to leadership in the church. To rectify this, Christians must both confess the harm we've caused and change our approach to sin.

Not only does this weaponized approach to sin cause unnecessary suffering among people; it distorts a healthy understanding of sin that could help us walk in faithfulness. You see, one Greek word used for *sin* (ἁμαρτία—transliterated *hamartia*) actually comes from ancient archery. It means "to miss the mark." Any shot that wasn't a bull's-eye was a sin. The shot went awry, and the archer needed to adjust their aim to hit the target. Correcting your behavior so you don't miss a target isn't about upholding someone else's subjective sense of purity but instead about taking the path best oriented toward your goal.

Discernment in vocational exploration recognizes that many paths are available, and some of them will lead us to miss our intended mark or at least make the journey much more difficult. This means that discernment takes sin seriously, not out of a desire to shame others or to demean ourselves, but instead out of a fierce commitment to the idea that the target, abundant life, is worth shooting for. After all, our definition of *vocation* is any meaningful, life-giving work for the world. So what's meaningful for me might miss the mark for other people. And while we all can participate in God's abundant life, how that abundance is manifested for one person might miss the mark for others. Discernment means taking seriously what's meaningful for ourselves and life-giving for the people we serve as we evaluate the options we've discovered.

Let's consider, just for a moment, this concept of abundant life. Many times throughout the book, I've referred to it and its origins in Jesus's teachings, but I haven't given you a clear definition thus far. In some ways, it's easy to talk about. Abundant life is life that isn't marred by sin, that isn't diminished by suffering, that isn't tormented by oppression, that isn't ruined by racism. In short, abundant life is the life we would have if sin weren't in the picture. What that looks like is not clear to us, since sin's presence is still painfully obvious. So there's some mystery to the concept of abundant life.

Yet in earlier chapters, I said that activating our vocations involves a kind of time travel. To embrace our purpose, to live out our vocation, is time travel because it brings the future into the present and offers us a glimpse of holy perfection. That's what abundant life looks like, making clear the presence of heaven here on the earth. That's the mark we're aiming for as we assess our priorities. What is it that I do that doesn't dwell in sin but, instead, makes the presence of eternity palpable?

But how do you discern the mark you're aiming at in the first place? How do you evaluate the importance of your different skills and passions? How do you prioritize the potential vocations in your life? Fortunately, there are some tangible practices you can put to use in your own life.

Discernment Practices

Since discernment is the process of prioritizing your discoveries, discernment practices should help you clarify what your priorities are. There are many ways you can go about this process. Some seem quite straightforward, while others appear a bit mystical, but the goal of any discernment practice is ultimately for you to understand your priorities in ways that help make clear what work might be meaningful and life-giving for you.

Asset Mapping

One way to identify synergy between internal and external calls is through a process called asset mapping. I employ this process frequently with students, in both individual coaching sessions and group meetings, to discern possible futures. Asset mapping can be used in many ways, but the strategy that follows is designed specifically for vocational exploration.

You'll need something to write on and something to write with, preferably many different-colored writing utensils. If you are working with a group, use a large sheet so group members can see the map and you can take it with you after the group disperses.

Divide the sheet into three areas. Title the first one "What Assets Do I Have?" Though you might initially think of assets as primarily financial, those aren't the only resources you have available to you. Relationships are assets. Experiences are assets. Your living situation is an asset. Your language skills are assets, as are your educational experiences, your physical abilities, your knowledge, and your talents. Any resource that you can put to work is an asset.

Even if you aren't as good as others at something, that doesn't mean your ability isn't an asset. Few are as wealthy as Jeff Bezos, but we still have monetary assets at our disposal. Few are as athletic as LeBron James, but we can still have a love of the game and an ability to play. Few of us are as intelligent as Neil deGrasse Tyson, as well traveled as Rick Steves, as eloquent as Maya Angelou, as musically gifted as Beyoncé. Yet we all still have assets. An asset is still a resource even if it's not the best or the most. It's still an asset if it's not perfect. It's an asset because it's yours and you're able to use it for something beyond yourself.

With that in mind, write in this first section as many assets—resources you have at your disposal—as you can think of. If you have trouble naming specific assets, return to the list of examples to see what might inspire you.

Then title the second area "What Are My Values?" In this section, write down the things that are most important to you. This list is significant because the things you value shape your purpose. For instance, if you value the environment, then at least one of your vocations will likely connect with the outdoors. Ask questions like "What fundamental values shape the way I live?" and "What key commitments inform my worldview?" Thinking about your values helps connect your specific passions and the greater transcendent purpose you serve. In other words, it helps make clear the cosmic significance of specific vocations. Some of your values might be rooted in your faith tradition; you might even think of these as God's values. But if you claim them as your own, include them on your sheet. However you understand ultimate meaning, the reason we exist, the meaning of life, put the underlying values in this section.

Then move to the third area and title it "What Unmet Needs Do I See?" After all, if vocation is any meaningful, life-giving work for the world, then that work is going to be meeting needs that you notice in the world in which you live. Of course, you might be aware of an overwhelming number of needs, so begin by focusing on those most obvious to you. These might be abstract, like "compassion" or "purpose," or specific, like "affordable housing in downtown Seattle" or "clean water in the Global South." These are the needs that you notice, that pique your interest, that you feel compelled to consider or responsible to address.

Here's one of the most important aspects of asset mapping: it's almost always enriched when other people are a part of the process. Some people see assets in you that you don't see in yourself. Your friends might remember a conversation with you in which you named a specific need in the world or expressed a particular worldview that doesn't quickly come to your mind. You're in control of the process, so if someone names something that isn't a need you're passionate about or that doesn't reflect your values or how you understand God's values, you can always say no. Yet the conversation itself might inspire more reflection on your assets, values, and sense of the world's needs.

When you've run out of responses to the three questions, start to make connections across the areas. How do the assets you possess relate to the needs you see in the world and the values you've identified? What potential vocations—not just careers but meaningful, life-giving work in any realm of life—might bring together your assets with holy purpose to satisfy the hungers of the world? Use different colors to circle the related content or create webs so you can begin to envision how these different themes can come together to create a substantial story line in your life.

As the name suggests, asset mapping can be an invaluable tool for you to navigate the maps you create as you explore your vocations. As you clarify connections between assets, values, and needs, you can begin to see a path that connects your assets to the world's needs through your shared values. In those places, you just may find a vocation.

Priority Matrix

Another helpful tool to discern the value of things in your life is a priority matrix. One relatively famous model is President Dwight Eisenhower's urgency and importance matrix. When giving a speech in 1954 to the Second World Council of Churches, Eisenhower commented that he had two kinds of problems to deal with: the urgent and the important. He further observed that not all urgent problems are important and that not all important problems are urgent. Importance is based on priorities, both your own and those for whom you work. Urgency is another word for time bound. Some things need to be completed by a certain time in order to be successful. Thus was born the urgency and importance matrix. While many forms of this matrix exist, they all contain the elements shown in figure 7.1.

This matrix can be helpful for making decisions about immediate issues. Consider, for instance, that you have an exam tomorrow that you have not yet studied for, and you also have a friend you've spent a lot of time with lately who invites you to go have a few drinks at a local bar. Since your role as a friend and your role as a student are both

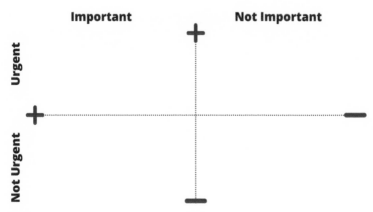

Figure 7.1: *Urgency and importance matrix*

vocations, they're fairly close in importance. But given that you've spent lots of time with this friend lately and the immediacy of the test, studying is a more urgent manner. You've discerned the value of your possibilities, so you can decide what to do.

However helpful this matrix is for weighing decisions about vocations you already know are yours, this matrix can't always help you decide whether you want to pursue another vocation. Another kind of matrix that can help move the needle on your vocational options is a value versus matrix. Versions of this are often used in corporations. You can set it up with a variety of comparisons: Value versus risk. Value versus complexity. Value versus cost. Each of these can help you see the value of options compared to other options as well as how that value relates to other factors. That matrix would look something like what is shown in figure 7.2.

So imagine you're weighing whether to become a welder, a pilot, or a physician's assistant (PA). While different vocations, each relate to the STEM (science, technology,

Figure 7.2: *Value versus matrix: value versus risk/cost/ complexity*

engineering, and math) fields and have higher earning potentials, even at entry-level positions. How you evaluate those potential careers might include factors such as the amount and kind of contact you want with other people, from relatively little as a welder, to lots of surface relationships with many passengers daily as a pilot, to deeper knowledge of a smaller group of people's personal lives as a PA. It might also include a desire to make something tangible with your hands, or to travel, or to see the personal impacts of your work on the lives of others.

You can then weigh the risk of each vocational option to your physical health, your familial relationships, the time you invest in other vocations, and the like. Or you might assess the cost to obtain the required education compared to the potential income it can produce. Or you evaluate the complexity of pursuing that vocation and whether you consider the necessary investment wise stewardship of your time and resources. Overall, how easy would it be for you—not others, with their skills and passions, but you—to fulfill this vocation? Laying those determinations out on a grid can give you a visualization of what feels internally muddled.

Let's consider our examples based on the investment of time and money in the acquisition of necessary degrees and certifications. You could lay out a coordinate plane like figure 7.3 and then plot, based on your discoveries, how much you'd have to invest in order to become a welder, a pilot, or a PA. To become a welder takes as little as seven months or up to two years and can often be acquired through apprenticeships or community college programs that require little personal investment or that pay you while you are in training. To become a commercial pilot also takes about two years, or fifteen hundred hours of flying, but it costs tens of thousands of dollars. To become a PA, you must earn a bachelor's degree and then spend three more years in classes and certification, a process that can cost more than one hundred thousand dollars. How you value each of those possible careers is more subjective. Your rankings might ultimately be different from those of another person

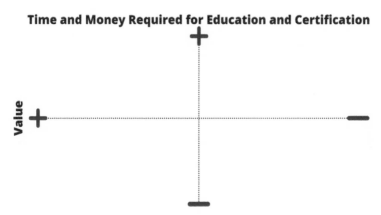

Figure 7.3: *Value versus matrix: value versus required investments*

evaluating the same options. Even so, putting it all together on such a chart can help you compare the options in more tangible ways.

Although I've worked with many students who have found this matrix useful, I acknowledge that the process can feel somewhat mechanical. Some people feel this approach reduces the discernment of vocation to simple math rather than recognizing a calling from beyond ourselves. If you're feeling that way, that's totally fine. This tool may not be for you. The more organic approach of asset mapping may prove more fruitful.

One way I've modified the priority matrix is by fusing it with the definition for vocation, so instead of language that rings more like corporate finance, it puts the spectrums of meaningful and life-giving into a matrix, as seen in figure 7.4.

While vocation doesn't have to be meaningful for just me or life-giving only for others, framing it this way helps me keep in mind that I'm a part of a larger community, that my vocation's impact extends beyond myself even as

Figure 7.4: *Value versus matrix: meaningful for me versus life-giving for others*

it is deeply connected to me. If you can't imagine how an option might be life-giving for others, perhaps invite a few friends to reflect with you on that. If it's not life-giving for others, then it's probably not a vocation for you. Similarly, if you can't find meaning in the work—either for yourself or for others, and either existential, personal meaning or meaning that meets immediate needs—then it's probably not your vocation.

We might use this matrix to weigh other factors. For example, a friend once wrote an article about vocation as doing work that needs to be done, even if it's not exciting work.[1] This valuable perspective is a way to frame vocation without getting obsessed with enjoyment, and I like that a lot. Framing vocation in terms of need, though, depends on how we understand what "needs" to be done. Who gets to define what is necessary? Sometimes we're asked to do work that doesn't need to be done—by anyone. This busywork, paper shuffling, isn't vocation. Some tasks are dirty, thankless grunt work but are necessary and therefore life-giving. Cleaning toilets, servicing septic tanks, and changing diapers all come to mind. This work needs to be done to ensure our communities are sanitary; it is life-giving because it keeps us free from disease. No work that truly needs to be done lacks meaning. It may not be considered profound by many, but it is meaningful nonetheless. For our definition, and using this matrix, we define what's meaningful and life-giving work for the world in conversation with our communities and our faith traditions. We can determine together that a work is not particularly meaningful, but because it is necessary, it is life-giving and therefore a vocation to which someone might be called. You, created in the image of God, in conversation with others who are also images of God, can assess whether the work truly is a vocation—at least for someone, if not you. That's discernment.

Meditating on the Possible

Even with all these tools available—the conceptual maps alongside asset mapping and priority matrixes—it's important to remember that discernment is not the end of the journey. Some options, even those identified through careful discernment, might seem exciting to others but not obviously relate to your passions. Others won't thrill you but seem necessary or significant for some reason. I encourage you to pay attention to your internal response to options you discern and explore them through deep, intentional meditation.

One of the most important books I've read on prayer is by a neuroscientist and a therapist. *How God Changes Your Brain* is a deceptive title. In fact, it's really a misnomer, because it's not about God at all. Instead, it's a book about how any form of prayer or meditation can have long-term effects on the ways our brains function, which can in turn have significant impacts on our personalities. If you've never had that experience, I encourage you to read the book.[2]

I mention it not because of the science but because it points to the power meditation has to help all people be more deeply aware of themselves and the wider world. The authors found that in just seven to twelve minutes of meditation or prayer a day, people experience not only more peace and less anxiety within themselves but more compassion for and greater awareness of the world around them. Extensive research across religious traditions has shown that meditation can help people grow in confidence, appreciation, and clarity about themselves and about the world around them—all valuable qualities as we explore what we're called to do. Spiritual practices, then, offer another path to vocational discernment. Choose to pause and reflect, to focus on the present moment and discern where your heart leads. Even if your discernment seems to contradict your learnings from asset mapping and value matrixes, you are still gathering information to help you activate your vocations.

I've included a short script for meditation in case you've never practiced it before. Here are a few pointers for preparing: First, as much as is possible, remove distractions. Put your smartphone on "Do Not Disturb." Turn off your computer's notifications. Put a "Do Not Knock" note on your door. We can't truly block out all distractions, which you'll see in the script, but we can carve out some space for meditation. Second, set a timer for the period you plan to meditate. If this is your first experience with meditation, I suggest five minutes. Choose a soothing, lower-volume alarm rather than a jarring gong. Finally, select a seat that will be comfortable for the time you plan to meditate, yet not so comfortable that you're tempted to fall asleep. For instance, I might use a cushion on the floor, but if I sit on a soft chair, I usually move to the edge to force myself to remain upright and attentive throughout the meditation process. If you think reading and meditating at the same time might be distracting, I encourage you to use your cell phone and record the following meditation, slowly, in your own voice. Then play the recording, allowing yourself to focus on the practice itself.

Now, I invite you to close your eyes if you're comfortable doing so. If not, choose a neutral point in the room to focus your gaze on, perhaps the corner of the ceiling and wall. Take a deep breath in through your nose and out through your mouth, filling your lungs to full capacity. Again, in through your nose and out through your mouth. Once more, breathe in and out.

Let your breath return to normal and take note of how you feel. Scan from your head to neck and torso, out to each of your limbs, down to your toes, and notice any comfort or discomfort in your body. Be aware of the sensations. Acknowledge them. Then set them aside.

Now take note of the thoughts in your mind, the things that seek your attention. Be aware of them. Acknowledge them. Then set them aside.

Continue to allow your breath to rise and fall naturally, giving thanks for this natural rhythm, the in-taking of life.

Now bring to mind two options you're considering as vocations. Begin with one. Express gratitude that it is possible for you to consider this call. Then imagine yourself inhabiting this vocation. How do you feel when performing the tasks? Wearing the uniform? Using the tools? Embodying the role? Where do you find comfort or discomfort? What do you find exciting or troubling? What do you know about this calling now, and what is not yet clear? As you focus on this possibility, change your perspective. Assess the opportunity from other points of view. How does it relate to your identity? Your personality? Your spirituality? Offer thanks once more that you can consider this vocation and then set it aside.

Now bring to mind the other vocation you're considering. Imagine yourself inhabiting this vocation. How do you feel when performing the tasks? Wearing the uniform? Using the tools? Embodying the role? Where do you find comfort or discomfort? What do you find exciting or troubling? What do you know about this calling now, and what is not yet clear? As you focus on this possibility, change your perspective. Assess the opportunity from other points of view. How does it relate to your identity? Your personality? Your spirituality? Again, offer thanks once more that you can consider this vocation and then set it aside.

With those two considerations in mind, set a timer for five minutes. During this time, with each breath in and each breath out, simply state, "I am called to be." You might end that sentence with one of the options you just considered. Or other options might spark consideration. You might find that nothing fills the void. Notice if some options appear more frequently or inspire more positive energy. Whatever comes to mind is important information. Most important of all is to know that you are called to be. To exist. To take up this space, in this body, with this mind, and be. Embrace the silence. Breathe in. "I am called to be." Now breathe out. "I am called to be." Again and again, embracing the silence to reflect.

As the timer rings, bring your awareness back to your breath. Deeply breathe in, filling your lungs, then breathe out. Breathe in deeply again, and out. In once more, and release the air. As your breath returns to normal, remember to carry your reflections with you. Recall that you have options to consider, opportunities to embody, and most assuredly, a calling to be you in this place and at this time.

As you are comfortable, open your eyes to conclude your practice.

From Priorities to Practice

The resources given in the previous section are just a few applicable tools to equip you for discernment. Through asset mapping, priority matrixes, and meditation, you can not only interpret the map you are creating but evaluate how important each feature is as well as assess what kinds of vocations you're called to pursue. But priorities alone won't equip you to inhabit a calling. It is not simply enough to want to do meaningful, life-giving work for others. You must also learn how to do it. That's where development comes in, and development is where we turn next.

Chapter 8

Developing Your Skills

Do you know how a dolphin learns to fish? They practice. They work smart, work hard, and work together. And they play.

While staying at my aunt and uncle's condo in Southwest Florida, I wandered out to the tip of a peninsula to watch the sunset. Standing at the edge of the break wall, with waves gently lapping against the concrete, I suddenly heard crashing water, as though someone had fallen into the ocean. But there at my feet were two dolphins, an elder and a younger, splashing and zooming down the length of the condo complex. At first, they seemed to be just playing as the sun's final rays cast shadows from the mangroves across the bay. But as I looked closer, I saw them trapping fish against the wall, stunning them with their strong torsos, and then eating them with a quick gulp.

As you might expect, the younger dolphin wasn't as good as the elder. In their youthful jubilance, they certainly had more misses than hits. But the elder dolphin didn't stop the youth from trying. Instead, they shot in with experience and accuracy, made another catch, and then swam back to let the younger try again. They, indeed, were playing, but they were also practicing, especially the younger dolphin as they followed the lead of the elder.

But they weren't alone. Farther out in the bay, more fins peaked, the pod cresting the water as they pushed schools of fish toward the break wall. Even as the dolphins along the wall were working hard, the whole pod was working smart. Eventually, the two along the wall swam out to the bay, and a few others came closer to the edge to take their turn feeding. More hard work. More smart work. More practice. Together.

This is how we develop our skills. We practice and we play, working smart, working hard, and working together.

Development

As discernment helps you narrow the options you've discovered, development helps you hone the skills necessary for your potential vocations. Think about the extended free trial on the mattress you bought on the internet. You're trying out possibilities without fully committing. You're developing a sense of how you fit the mattress and the mattress fits you. If during a vocational trial you find that it's not a fit, that itself is a discovery that opens new possibilities. Perhaps, as you try to develop certain skills for particular vocations, you will find the work lacks meaning. That's OK. Perhaps you'll discover a limit to your potential for growth. That's fine. Part of the value of development is trying out possibilities and seeing whether any is truly a vocational fit. Remember, as you explore your vocational options, through discovery, discernment, and development, you can still say no to the opportunities at hand.

I can't overestimate the importance of rehearsal or the necessity of practice. What makes Tom Brady so annoyingly good at football isn't that he's the best athlete; it's that he's worked incredibly hard at practice to develop his skills and hone his diet and exercise to strengthen his body to outperform more natural athletes. And while you might assume I also learned the importance of practice from an athletic coach or a music professor, I didn't discover its value until I started reading Aristotle. Yes, this ancient philosopher is the one who instilled in me the vitality of practicing who I want to be.

Rest assured that coaches and teachers tried to instill the value of practice within me. They did so valiantly. My problem with practice, I found, wasn't the teachers. It was that, most often, I didn't find the activities meaningful enough to invest in the routine repetitions. I'm no Tom Brady (to no one's surprise), at least not when it comes to commitment to sports development. But that's because athletics aren't a primary vocation of mine.

Aristotle taught that every person is made for fulfillment, and to achieve this fulfillment, we must become virtuous people. For Aristotle, the key to becoming virtuous, and therefore finding fulfillment, was to continually put the virtues—things like justice, courage, humility, honesty, and wit—into practice. In his view, we can't just decide to become courageous. We must act with courage, and over time, we will become courageous people. To become who we are meant to be, Aristotle thought, we must practice those things most essential to human flourishing and form them as habits until they become second nature to us.

So, too, practicing your vocation can help you inhabit human flourishing. You don't just decide to become a chef or an optometrist or a boat captain. You practice the things associated with those vocations in order to become those things. So aspiring chefs try new dishes. Potential optometrists take anatomy and physiology courses. Captains in training pilot a boat under the guidance of accomplished sailors. All these activities are done to make a habit out of their vocations.

This notion of habit highlights the importance of the phrase *second nature*. Remember that our vocations are not our identities, so they're not our first nature. But by practicing the things essential to the vocations we're considering, we can make them second nature. So my identity is not as an administrator. The work doesn't come naturally to me. But over time, I've found that administration helps me live my mission—to empower others to clarify their identities and develop their vocations. This doesn't mean I'm excellent at it yet—just ask the students who work for me—but over time, I've developed habits that enable me to support them as they discern and develop (and yes, discover and decide) who they're called to be and what they're called to do.

Following the Leader and Leading into Your Purpose

How do we know what we need to do in order to develop our skills? We follow the examples set by those who excel in those areas. Aristotle says that to become virtuous, it's helpful to emulate the actions of people who are known to be virtuous.

While I didn't find myself enamored of the examples of my athletic coaches, many others' excellent examples inspired me to develop my own skills as I grew in my vocations. As a musician, Dave Cottrell taught me how to play drums not just by giving me weekly lessons but by conveying exuberance as he sat behind a sparkling blue Ludwig drum kit. At one of the loneliest moments in my life, Karen Wayt and Barb Brown showed me how to love even through the most difficult times. Willie James Jennings modeled how to teach with sympathy for students and a commitment to justice. Esther

Acolatse embodied how to be a compassionate pastor and a rigorous academic. Thulie Beresford exemplified how to be a campus pastor with drive, determination, and joy. Preachers like Rick Lischer and Leah Schade shaped my proclamation. Following in the footsteps of leaders like these, practicing what they displayed, helped me embrace different vocations and realize that some options just didn't fit.

You may know some of the names I just mentioned. Others likely ring no bells for you. That's OK, because a key to each of my examples, a key not necessarily inherent in Aristotle's thought, is that all these connections are personal. Teachers and mentors, family and friends, the exemplars who weren't untouchable in their celebrity but instead intimate in their proximity—they all modeled for me the ways I could practice my vocations. Now, of course, I have learned significantly from people I don't know. How can I listen to Otis Moss III's sermons and not learn?[1] But the personal connections allow me to learn not just public tactics but the daily embodiment that enables me to publicly live out my vocations. Following the leaders close to us helps us form those vocational habits because they're a more frequent part of our lives.

Think, then, about the potential vocations you've discovered, especially the ones you've discerned are significant options in your life, and of course, the vocations you already inhabit. Who are the people in your life who do these things well? What personal connections do you have with people who do this work in meaningful, life-giving ways for others? Once you've identified these people, one way to develop your skills is to emulate them—to work the way that they work, to prepare the way that they prepare. For instance, student musicians who want to play more like a certain artist often research the kind of gear that artist plays on as well as explore the practice methods the artist prefers. By emulating this accomplished artist, the students become more competent in their potential calling. More than one sage has said, "We make the road by walking," which is most certainly true, and we learn to walk by following in others' footsteps. Pay close attention to those who set positive examples. Ask about their routines. With their permission, record notes of how you can develop through practice the skills that you see these mentors embody.

One danger we face when following the actions of others is the belief that to take hold of our vocation, we must become someone else. I spoke of this danger in chapter 1, where I wrote about trying to become someone else rather than learning how my identity relates to my vocations. My attempts to do so poisoned my path for a time. A wiser strategy as we learn about vocations from the positive examples set by others is to personalize our vocation in ways that align with our identities and reflect our personalities—to become more mindful of how we learn from others without becoming someone else. We can both learn best practices from others and become our best selves.

This requires an incredible intentionality, but by this point, you're already equipped with some of the tools to realize the needed self-awareness. Practices such as meditation, which increase both your self-perception and awareness of others, provide strong scaffolding for this work. Asset mapping, alongside communities that recognize your skills and challenges, helps highlight how what you do relates to who you are. All grounded in your faith or worldview, the sense that there is holy purpose within you—because there's a cosmic spark, a transcendent breath, a divine image within each of us—empowers you to embrace yourself as you embrace your purpose. That takes practice. Fortunately, a number of other activities are available to help you develop your skills in ways that are authentic to you, even as you follow others who've practiced your vocation before you.

Practices for Your Development

Contrary to the cliché, practice doesn't make perfect. We're human, after all, so perfection is out of our reach. Practice can't make us perfect, but it can sure make us better. Research published by the American Association of Colleges and Universities shows that "high-impact practices" increase student persistence and engagement in the educational process.[2] In short, a high-impact practice is an action that correlates with higher graduation rates, GPAs, and other marks of college student persistence. Perhaps most important, high-impact practices benefit students from many backgrounds, not just the economically or culturally privileged. Two high-impact practices have significant potential to help you develop skills as you explore possible vocations.

Internships have a long history in vocational exploration. Sometimes called fieldwork, field education, field placements, learning in context, leadership in context, student teaching, vicarage, or a host of other terms, internships provide a chance to perform the work one thinks they're called to do alongside professionals in the field. Many inequities exist in the realm of internships, as hosts sometimes view them as a source of unpaid labor, and some lack specific goals or effective supervisors. Even with those issues in mind, students who participate in internships have better GPAs and graduation rates than those who don't engage in those opportunities.

An internship is an invaluable way for you to try the vocation on with the safety net of knowledgeable guides and a timeline that allows you to step out without negative impacts on the community you're working with. For instance, I know students who discovered they were not called to be teachers during their student teaching placements. I also know many others who only realized their potential once they were embedded in a classroom. In fact, one of my favorite stories of this experience comes from Samantha DiBiaso, a former graduate assistant who worked in my office.

Samantha and I met while I was her pastor at The Well, Virginia Tech's Lutheran Campus Ministry. As she graduated, I encouraged her to consider attending seminary, because I experienced in her unique gifts for transformational leadership, something our denomination sorely needs. At that time, she was unsure about her path and instead chose to participate in a gap year program. After a year of service in South Africa with the ELCA's Young Adults in Global Mission, Samantha eventually chose to attend Trinity Lutheran Seminary at Capital University and become a graduate assistant in Capital's Center for Faith and Learning. Through her work with undergraduate students planning worship and leading them through a global pandemic, she realized her call was to be a pastor who encouraged people, through worship, to pursue justice for God's creation outside of the traditional structures of the church. It was Samantha's internship-like gap experience with Young Adults in Global Mission that led her to realize a call to become a seminary student. It was Samantha's field placement in campus ministries that led her to claim her call to become a pastor.

Internships are powerful ways to clarify what you are and are not called to do. High school and college students have access to these experiences through career development, community engagement, and other similar offices. (Ask an advisor or counselor where to find more information.) If you're not a student, you'll need to be a bit more proactive in seeking opportunities. Be bold enough to ask those in arenas you feel called to consider if there's a place for you to learn alongside them. Also check online job sites, as many also list internship opportunities.

Often less formal but no less important, service learning is another high-impact practice that increases student success. Also called community engagement or community-engaged learning, this approach to work outside the classroom attempts to avoid one-off events that often describe community service. Instead, service learning seeks to foster long-term relationships with community partners in schools, businesses, religious centers, neighborhoods, and nonprofit organizations. It also matches the vocational possibilities of students with the needs of their partners. The goal is to foster systemic change within or through the organization the student is serving and to provide a lasting, formative relationship of mutuality for the students involved.

Community-engaged learning isn't just about the student or volunteer but about how their experiences and gifts benefit others too. Unlike a one-time mission trip, such a model entails a long-term relationship between their organization and the communities they visit. Providing more than photo ops in schools or hospitals, community-engaged learning involves a commitment to an established program, such as America Reads and America Counts or a volunteer position in a medical center. Rather than offering a chance to do things that make a student feel good, these programs match their skills with the opportunities available.

If you're a college student, such opportunities are growing on most campuses in North America, so seek them out. If you're not, check in with local nonprofits, religious communities, and civic associations to see what opportunities might be available for you. You don't need to take just any opportunity that arises. Instead, you can choose a service-learning relationship that can help you develop skills related to your vocational possibilities and be a blessing to the community with which you work.

Though not identified in high-impact practice research, another emerging trend in higher education is to gamify the classroom—to create games that also are opportunities to build knowledge or skills. In grade school, we used to play a game called "Around the World" in social studies. Mr. Anderson would have us toss a ball to different classmates to answer questions related to the topic we'd been studying. The goal was for everyone to answer at least one question correctly. It turned learning into a team game where nobody won until everybody won. Other resources, like Kahoot!, Quizlet, and Jamboard, allow for real-time engagement either in person or remotely to add game elements to review and ideation sessions (a process for generating ideas).

One of the dangers of the development phase of vocational formation is that we might treat opportunities like obligations rather than life-giving possibilities. Gamifying your experience can reduce that sense of duty. You can identify goals for the experience and offer yourself rewards for achieving them. Use tools like internships, community-engaged learning, and gamified education to reinforce the knowledge necessary for the work. Invite others with similar interests or skills to participate with you to increase the team experience.

One of the reasons this approach is helpful is that it can reveal your level of investment in what you're doing. If you realize you enjoy the game but do not find the content meaningful, then the arena in which you are playing is probably not your vocation. On the other hand, if you find yourself so enamored of the work's purpose that you don't need a game to stay involved, then that speaks volumes to the vocational priority for you.

Development and Direction

Vocation isn't random. It comes from somewhere and it appears through effort. Sometimes such efforts can feel unintentional, but that doesn't mean you didn't try to develop some habits; it just means the work was fun or that it came naturally to you. At other times, and for many people, development requires very specific effort. The aforementioned practices can help focus that attention and direct your activity. When combined with the work of discernment, prioritizing the opportunities available for you, development can become an exciting pilgrimage rather than a trudge through the muck. To develop your skills, to practice, doesn't have to feel monotonous or unnecessary. You can do it with a team. You can make an explicit impact on others. What matters most is your reflection on the meaning of your effort.

With discovery, discernment, and development in action, one last disposition comes into play for your vocation search: decision. That's where we now turn.

Chapter 9

Deciding What's Next

I can't tell you how many times, as a kid and as an adult, I've had some version of this conversation:

"Hey, what do you want to do for lunch?"
They respond with some form of "Whatever."

Here's another:

"Hey, what do you want to do this afternoon?"
They reply with some version of "I don't care."

Sometimes for a few minutes, sometimes for a much more unreasonable amount of time, we delay decisions because we seem to have some significant social aversion to choosing. All over a simple meal or a recreational activity.

But here's the thing: we all know that often, "I don't care" is a lie and "Whatever" is patently false. If you ask me where I want to eat and I state no preference, you should know that I feel about Burger King the same way that Jon Stewart feels about Arby's and my wife feels about thin-crust pizza. Not fans, to put it mildly. Many of us have preferences we don't vocalize at the time. There's certainly a preference within us, but for some reason, when asked for our inclination, we all too often avoid clarity.

This isn't just a common social aversion, though. Some faith traditions also have a theological aversion to decisions, at least certain kinds of decisions. While people in some Christian circles ask if you've "accepted Jesus as your Lord and Savior" or if you've "decided to let God into your heart," that question is quite alien to others, including me. You might remember that from my discussion of God's mission a few chapters ago, where I write about the biblical witness that God is at work reconciling all things. Reconciliation is God's work, God's choice—indeed, God's vocation. For me, then, some decisions properly belong to God rather than to me or other people. While this aversion to "decision theology" often arises from a valuable theological perspective, it can become an overcorrection that makes people like me averse to all decisions.

Decision avoidance occurs in other religious traditions and cultures, perhaps including yours, perhaps for different reasons. When faced with choices, we often attempt to remain neutral, to not choose anything, so as not to rock the boat or cause conflict. Of course, as Elie Wiesel reminds us, neutrality isn't really possible when options exist. Speaking of anti-Judaism and apartheid in his Nobel Prize acceptance speech, Wiesel said, "We must take sides. Neutrality helps the oppressor, never the victim. Silence encourages the tormentor, never the tormented. Sometimes we must interfere."[1] To be clear, not every situation is as grievous as the Holocaust or European colonialism. Still, Wiesel's wisdom applies broadly. To not choose is a choice—a choice to remain the same or at least a commitment to complacency. That is why decisions are so difficult for those with privilege or power. To choose change is to risk the comfort we might currently experience, to challenge the way things are. And yet, not choosing can also be a choice to let the status quo continue to do its damage. That decision is passive participation in harm rather than promotion of abundant life. We need to realign the conversation on decisions to hit the mark of meaningful, life-giving work.

What we need, religiously and societally, is to reclaim the power of decisions, recognizing their value and their limits.

Reframing Decisions

Some people seem to think they're forever bound to the decisions they make, but that's not true. We can make one decision and then choose to make another decision that contradicts or even negates the previous decision. Decisions are not eternal. At least, they don't need to last forever.

Savanna Sullivan, currently the program executive for youth at the Lutheran World Federation, introduced me to the idea that when we make vocational decisions, we choose our "next most faithful step."[2] This approach came from her participation with the Forum for Theological Exploration (FTE). I found this out for myself as a partner at an FTE event and as I read *Another Way: Living and Leading Change on Purpose*, a fantastic book written by a cohort of FTE alumni and partners. This resource, designed for community discernment, is excellent and bears significant wisdom for our personal vocational exploration. In short, we can acknowledge that choices are not forever. Rather, we can view any decision as one aspect of a faithful journey, an approach that allows us to appreciate the value of any particular course of action without giving any choice too much influence in our lives.

Of course, decisions have consequences. And we can't unmake a decision. But we can address consequences with other choices, and we can choose to step in a different direction if we're unhappy with how the last decision played out. Christian ethicist Cynthia Moe-Lobeda uses similar logic when addressing the climate crisis in her book *Resisting Structural Evil: Love as Ecological-Economic Vocation.* Rather than approach climate problems as too expansive to change, Moe-Lobeda emphasizes the fact that human decisions have resulted in the impacts we are experiencing, and so humans can choose to make other impacts. Moe-Lobeda isn't naive to the scope of the issue and points to the need for national and global choices as well as individual decisions. But we need not let the reality of negative consequences keep us from making bold decisions, because we are capable of making other decisions to reorient us toward our target, to repent and try again.[3]

Each of these leaders highlights that decisions are important, but they are not always permanent. Decisions are not gods we worship; rather, they are actions we take. Decisions are not San Diego weather or the North Pole, apparently fixed. Decisions, like Appalachian leaves, will change with the seasons. Colors will shift, fibers will dry, old leaves will fall, and in time, new leaves grow with new verdancy. Let's think about how the seasonal nature of decisions relates to decisions specifically about vocations.

A Time for Everything

If you've been to a Christian wedding or funeral, the odds are high that you've heard a reading from Ecclesiastes 3 that says there's a time for everything. War and peace. Planting and harvesting. Weeping and laughing. Silence and speech. Mourning and dancing. The writer of such wisdom doesn't say these experiences are all good or easy but rather reminds readers that all are experiences of life, and all are temporary.

I think about decisions in a similar way. There is a time for decisions about college and career, relationships and finances, meals and housing, purchasing and saving, work and recreation. That doesn't mean all these decisions are easy; rather, each time of life has associated decisions. You don't need to decide everything right now. Elementary schoolers don't need to settle on a career. Middle schoolers don't need to decide how many children they will have one day or whether they'll have children at all. High schoolers don't need to choose a retirement location. In other words, we can focus on the decisions that matter most right now. If we refrain from saturating ourselves with unnecessary decisions, we will find more time and energy to invest in the decisions that matter most today.

We also do not need to dwell on past decisions. A choice you regret from ten years ago may have shaped your future, but there's nothing you can do a decade later to change that except make different decisions now. You can be grateful for a decision in your childhood that positively shaped your life, but too much focus on that past success can distract you from making similarly significant decisions today. Of course, we can and should learn from the decisions we've made in the past in ways that inform our current decisions. We just shouldn't live in the past in ways that make us miss the present.

We do need to recognize that different decisions have different significance. What we decide to eat for lunch and where we decide to go to college have different price tags and impacts on our lives. Where we choose to live affects our lives differently from where we choose to vacation. Deciding to mow the lawn is certainly different from choosing to harvest a field. That's another value of the discernment and development tools I shared earlier. A priority matrix can help us visualize whether the decision we're focused on is worth the time we're giving it or as urgent as it feels. As we evaluate how the pieces of our lives fit together, we can also give appropriate weight to the associated decisions. Giving the proper amount of effort and investment to a decision, in its time, can decrease our anxiety about the decision itself and instead enable us to live in the moment as we do meaningful, life-giving work for others. We don't need to give minor decisions major space in our brains or let yesterday's or tomorrow's choices distract from today's priorities.

Resources for Decisions

If you're looking for a neat, linear decision-making process, prepare to be disappointed. As you've seen throughout the book, vocational exploration isn't tidy or linear. That's one reason why the formation process I describe is 4D. Just as you live life in all dimensions at the same time, so too you explore your vocations simultaneously through discoveries, discernment, development, and decisions. But just because there is no step-by-step process doesn't mean no resources exist to help you make decisions. In fact, we've discussed many at length already. Let's review.

First, as you feel ready to make a decision about a vocation, assess how it relates to your identity. Does it accurately align with who you are? Can you keep your identity differentiated from this vocation? Resources such as asset mapping can help you evaluate this as well as how well a vocation can allow you to put your identity, passions, and resources to work for others.

Relatedly, do you view the work as meaningful? If you've gone through discernment and development, you should have relevant experience to draw on as you reflect. Even if the work lacks joy for you, do you sense a greater purpose to it? Do you see that it needs to be done because it brings relief or meets others' needs? Do others experience it as life-giving? These questions suggest why internships and service learning are so important. They enable you to try the vocation on for size before you take a more determined step.

Another question to address is whether you experience an internal and an external call to this work. Are you feeling an inward tug and receiving outer affirmation that this could be your next most faithful step? Resources such as community feedback, mentor wisdom, and internship evaluations will help you comprehend the outer call. Meditation or prayer that promotes mindfulness and self-awareness will enable you to determine the inner call.

Your community—and in particular, those closest to you, those you trust to tell you the truth even if you don't want to hear it—is an essential testing ground for potential decisions as well. You don't want to turn to people who will tell you "You can do anything you put your mind to," because that's patently untrue. I could not be an NBA basketball player, a nuclear physicist, or a mother. In those cases, I lack the requisite skills, interests, and gender identity, respectively. Instead, you want to ask people who will critically engage the question of vocation with you, appraising your assets, evaluating your opportunities, and ensuring you've prioritized options and practiced in ways that properly prepare you for this next most faithful step. Share the decision you're considering with close confidants and ask for honest feedback. Their responses can provide vital information as you approach the next step.

The Quaker tradition, formally known as the Religious Society of Friends, utilizes a practice called clearness committees to guide decision-makers, including vocational explorers. The member will bring an issue—in this case, a decision related to possible vocation—to a trusted group of fellow Quakers. Rather than decide for the explorer, a clearness committee instead asks evocative questions to ensure the explorer is making a decision for the right reasons. You, too, could gather a group of trusted confidants who can ask compassionate, direct questions to test your confidence in the decision at hand. Parker Palmer writes about this process in *A Hidden Wholeness*.[4]

Decisions and Accountability

Perhaps another reason people seem to fear decisions is that they're concerned about the associated responsibility. If we publicly claim a decision, whether it's about a restaurant or a political candidate or a vocation, then we also identify ourselves as responsible, at least in part, for the results of that decision. That's not so bad when people like the decision, but if they don't? Conflict, perhaps even shame, seems to be right around the corner. That's one of the reasons I suggest being intentional about the significant decisions in our lives, especially the vocational choices we make. We want to be sure that a decision is one we're willing to be responsible for.

When we are willing to accept accountability for our decisions, we can more easily admit mistakes, take responsibility for failure, or apologize for pain caused. That outcome might seem strange at first, but think about it this way: if you're aware of how responsible you are, you're also aware of where your accountability ends. Specificity here can be liberating. When you say specifically what you're sorry for, you don't also take on others' faults. In a small example, imagine you chose where you and a friend will eat dinner, and your friend gets food poisoning there. Is it your fault that they got food poisoning and you didn't? Of course not. You didn't give them food poisoning or choose their food. But you can make new choices in light of that information. You can choose to eat elsewhere next time.

In the realm of vocation, you might choose a path that has conflict associated with it. While you may not be responsible for the conflict's cause, entering that vocation does give you a responsibility to address it. For instance, a number of people carry a distaste of Christian clergy because of the abuse, theft, and bigotry committed by some pastors and priests—often in God's name or through the manipulation of Scripture and theology. Though I did not do those things, I can apologize for the hurt caused by churches and their leaders. Though I didn't cause the harm, the effects are real and shape people's engagement with my vocation. I can also choose to structure my vocation in such a way that publicly promotes different behaviors and values. Addressing the damage done can help honor those whom I serve with my work by pursuing healing with integrity. A commitment to directly confronting the conflict within my vocation has been a major factor in my public advocacy for Black Lives Matter, Pride, and other groups often derided within the church.

You can also apologize for the ways you have caused harm. For instance, I did not always support the full inclusion of LGBTQ+ people in the church, much less serve as an ally. I confess that sin before you now just as I've confessed it in other communities for many years. It took the graceful, committed leading of queer Christians to help me see the harm I'd done and the false interpretations of Scripture that I relied on to support that prejudice. Taking responsibility for my past views is liberating because that honesty frees me for the relationships of reparation and, eventually, reconciliation. If you choose a vocation that includes conflict, you can also choose to model the kind of leadership that promotes healthy progress rather than avoids conflict altogether.

The beauty of taking responsibility for our decisions is that we can also be responsible for making different decisions. If you endeavor to become a professional musician but realize your inability to manage performance logistics makes you ill-suited for the competition in the field, you can decide on a new path. If you made a decision you regret, you can make a different decision in the future. That earlier journey, wherever it led you, was not a waste, for it revealed a truth to you—namely, that a certain calling wasn't for you. Yet you still carry with you the skills, relationships, and experiences from your time on that path, which in turn can prove useful for other vocations.

There's No Right Way

One of the most important contexts for decisions is this: there's no one right way, no objectively perfect path, to explore your vocation. Instead, the way you make with God is the right way to activate your purposes in this life.

Despite my constant refrain that this isn't a linear process, to offer four chapters on these four Ds may feel deceptive. You might feel tempted to start with discovery, then stop discovering so you can discern, then halt discernment so you can develop, then cease development once you decide what you're called to do.

But here's the thing: As you prioritize your options, you're likely to discover new ones. As you develop your skills, you're likely to discover new strengths. As you make decisions to pursue meaningful, life-giving work for others, their priorities may reshape your own, which will in turn lead to more discernment.

Vocational exploration is cyclical, a journey that constantly flows and swirls in overlapping layers. I imagine this interaction looking something like the four distinct Ds in figure 9.1. The crossroads in the middle is where discovery, discernment, development, and decision intersect. This

Figure 9.1: *An image of 4D Formation*

path reveals that, for example, even as you're focusing on development, you're constantly crossing opportunities to discover, discern, and decide. After intensive skill development, you will discover intriguing new options your entire life. Developing skills may lead you to value certain options more or less than before. Some decisions will require new discoveries, refreshed discernment, and renewed development. Exploring your vocation isn't a one-time event with a clean start and bow-tied end. Identifying your purposes is a lifelong process, and every decision can be a faithful step along that path.

I want to return to Aristotle for a minute. He believed that one becomes a virtuous person by practicing the actions of virtuous exemplars and making those practices habits. In other words, Aristotle's whole shtick—yes, I'm saying Aristotle had a shtick—was that we become virtuous by making our habits reflect virtues, such that our habits are consistently virtuous behaviors. I apply Aristotle's emphasis on habits to vocational exploration. You will become more mindful of the world in which you live if you habitually focus on the present—treating every moment as an opportunity for discovery. You will become more attuned to your values if you ritually evaluate your priorities. You will become more appreciative of your skills, and others' skills, as you undertake a practice regimen. And you will become more courageous as you take steps on the journey of clarifying your vocations, even into the uncertain, because you have discovered, developed, and discerned a call to that end.

Remember the wisdom of Zen master Dōgen (see chapters 1 and 4) that the truth is always available to us right now? Pema Chödrön, another Buddhist teacher, reframes the idea this way: "Every moment is an opportunity for awakening."[5] A mindful approach to our lives, one that takes note of the big and small things, can open us to a deeper knowledge of our environments, others, ourselves, and the sacred connection between all that undergirds our vocations. Through intentional participation in discovery, discernment, development, and decision, these behaviors can become habits that shape our whole lives.

This ancient wisdom to focus on the present is beautifully recast by FTE's encouragement to take the next most faithful step. Rather than try to get the journey right, we can focus on this moment, neither living in the past nor obsessing over the future but grateful for this step—a step informed by previous discoveries, discernment, development, and decisions. This step, one of sacred worth and holy opportunity, leads to new discoveries, discernment, development, and decisions. And the cycle goes on.

I'm not naive enough to think that every decision you make in your life requires enormous discoveries, extensive discernment, and laborious development. As I said before, ascribing the appropriate value to each decision helps you focus energy appropriately on the choices that truly require your attention. Yet a mindful approach to everyday decisions allows this set of tools to become a natural part of your life so that, when confusing or challenging situations arise, you're ready to deploy them in ways that breed confidence.

As we pursue vocation this way, we are neither obsessed with re-creating the steps others took nor determined to rush ahead without the wisdom of the past. With the tools I've mentioned along the way—using a map and a legend, reflecting on others' journeys and your own contributions, and following the stars that brighten your sky and a spiritual compass that reminds you of your true north—you can make choices that are informed by others yet suited to your specific identity and context. Your task is not to simply inhabit the journey that someone else walked. Instead, as you develop these habits, you're equipped to blaze your trail when new paths need to be made, even as you can also walk well-worn ways that still have value. Though you're not the first to perform your vocation, to do meaningful, life-giving work, you make your road by walking, step by faithful step.

From Dread to Determination

You are meant for meaningful, life-giving work in the world. Your vocations—career maven, engaged citizen, family member, environmental steward, and so many more—meet the needs of a world that needs you. You are significant. But remember, your decisions don't make you significant. Your identity, your belovedness, and your eternal worth exist prior to any work. Vocations are how you enact your value for the benefit of the world in which you live. Vocations, in putting your identity to work, are how you share yourself with the world that benefits just by getting to know you. You don't need to dread those decisions. Instead, you can make those decisions because you're worth meaningful, life-giving work, and so is the world in which you live. As you walk your path, commit yourself to being mindful of your environment, intentional with your relationships, focused in your priorities, purposeful in your practice.

This Is Not the End

Many books end with a conclusion, but as I've said, there is no conclusion to this process. You're constantly exploring your vocations. This book intends to help you do that with more self-awareness, more mindfulness, more intentionality, and more tools. So this is not a conclusion. This is a commissioning.

In Navajo circles, some people utilize a ritual called the Blessingway or Way Blessing Ceremony.[6] Rather than ask for the journey to be beautiful, the prayer acknowledges the beauty that already exists before and behind, above and below, truly all around. This way of blessing, rather than simply hoping for beauty, anticipates beauty. It acknowledges the sacred worth of you, others, and all creation, the divine spark that itself gives life to all creation. My sincere hope is that you notice the beauty all around and within you as you explore your vocations. The presence of beauty doesn't negate the challenges, ignore the evil, or dismiss the struggles. Rather, an awareness of the journey's beauty makes risking those things worthwhile. It fosters courage within you to take those faithful steps forward.

And that's what vocational exploration is for: finding the ways you will claim meaningful, life-giving work for others as your purpose. Through active discovery, reflective discernment, intentional development, and timely decisions, you can come to not only know what you're called to right now but also claim confidence in it for this season of the journey. You have tools—maps and legends, compasses and communities—that will prove useful as you explore. You're called with all of yourself, not despite yourself. And as you maintain a healthy differentiation between your identity and your vocations, you can remain certain of your worth and committed to transcendent purpose when your vocations change. That's what the theories and practices of the book can equip you to do—not just to realize a single vocation for one time but to continue to embrace vocations old and new throughout your life. That's what I commission you to do from here: intentional exploration of meaningful, life-giving work for all of your days. That is a journey from beauty to beauty, and I trust that sacred beauty will remain with you on all the paths ahead.

In my tradition, when someone departs our community to do specific work, we commission them. We read scripture, sing songs, partake in a holy meal, pray, share gifts, lay on hands as a sign of sending our energy and spirit with them, and utilize other rituals. As you depart from this reading, we can't share a meal together or otherwise physically commemorate the moment. I can, though, share with you a blessing, a prayer of good thoughts and best intentions that as you embark on this journey with new tools and perspectives, you would do so with courage. In fact, the blessing I share here is adapted from "The Prayer of Good Courage," which appeared in a mid-twentieth-century collection of prayers before it became a common feature in many worship books.[7] I frequently use some version of it at graduations, when we send students to continue their vocational exploration beyond the realms of classrooms and residence halls:

> May you know that you are called to meaningful, life-giving work for the world. In that, know that you are called to ventures of which we cannot see the ending, by paths as yet untrodden, through perils unknown. May you find faith to go out with good courage, trusting that you are worthy of the path before you. Though you know not precisely where you go, remember always that love goes before you, leading and supporting you in the great unknown. And, wherever you go and whatever you do, may you journey with beauty all the days of your life.

Notes

Chapter 1: God Calls You

1 Frederick Buechner, *Wishful Thinking: A Seeker's ABC* (San Francisco: HarperOne, 1993), 119.

2 Stephen Mitchell, "Dogen," in *The Enlightened Mind: An Anthology of Sacred Prose* (New York: HarperPerennial, 1993), 96–101.

3 See Wolfhart Pannenberg, *Theology and the Kingdom of God*, ed. Richard John Neuhaus (Philadelphia: Westminster Press, 1977).

Chapter 2: Defining Our Terms

1 "Beginning College Students Who Change Their Majors within 3 Years of Enrollment," National Center for Education Statistics, United States Department of Education, December 2017, https://nces.ed.gov/pubs2018/2018434 .pdf.

2 Jean M. Twenge et al., "Supplemental Material for Age, Period, and Cohort Trends in Mood Disorder Indicators and Suicide-Related Outcomes in a Nationally Representative Dataset, 2005–2017," *Journal of Abnormal Psychology* 128, no. 3 (2019): 185–99, https://doi.org/10.1037/abn0000410 .supp.

3 Sally C. Curtin and Melonie Heron, "Death Rates Due to Suicide and Homicide among Persons Aged 10–24: United States, 2000–2017," National Center for Health Statistics,

Centers for Disease Control and Prevention, October 2019, https://www.cdc.gov/nchs/data/databriefs/db352-h.pdf.

4   "Suicide Rising across the US," Vital Signs, Centers for Disease Control and Prevention, June 7, 2018, https://www.cdc.gov/vitalsigns/suicide/index.html.

5   Jeff Orlowski, dir. *The Social Dilemma*. Boulder, CO: Exposure Labs, 2020. 94 minutes. https://www.netflix.com/title/81254224.

6   For more, see George D. Kuh and Carol Geary Schneider, *High-Impact Educational Practices: What They Are, Who Has Access to Them, and Why They Matter* (Washington, DC: Association of American Colleges and Universities, 2008).

7   Makoto Fujimura, *Refractions: A Journey of Faith, Art, and Culture* (Colorado Springs: NavPress, 2009).

Chapter 3: You Are Called Wholly

1   Smalcald Articles 2.1.3. This is part of the larger set of Lutheran confessional documents, a collection of which can be found in Robert Kolb and Timothy J. Wengert, eds., *The Book of Concord: The Confessions of the Evangelical Lutheran Church* (Minneapolis: Fortress Press, 2000).

2   See, for instance, Rosalind Rosenberg, *Jane Crow: The Life of Pauli Murray* (New York: Oxford University Press, 2020).

Chapter 4: Called through Your Communities

1   Stanley Mack, *The Runaway Road* (New York: Parents Magazine Press, 1980).

2   *Jumu'ah* means "gathering day."

3   For more SBNR research, see Linda A. Mercadante, *Belief without Borders: Inside the Minds of the Spiritual but Not Religious* (New York: Oxford University Press, 2014).

4   Catherine M. Bell, *Ritual Theory, Ritual Practice* (New York: Oxford University Press, 1992), 197.

5   This quote, often mistakenly attributed to Joko Beck, appears in Joan Tollifson, *Awake in the Heartland: The Ecstasy of What Is* (Oakland, CA: Non-duality Press, 2006), 21.

6   "Song of Myself," sec. 51. Find the full text, along with an introduction to Whitman's work, in Walt Whitman and John Hollander, *Walt Whitman's Leaves of Grass* (New York: Penguin Random House, 2013).

7   See Andrew B. Newberg and Mark Robert Waldman, *How God Changes Your Brain: Breakthrough Findings from a Leading Neuroscientist* (New York: Ballantine Books, 2010).

Chapter 5: Called for Transcendent Mission

1   Aristotle, *Metaphysics*, trans. Hugh Lawson-Tancred (London: Penguin Books, 2004).

Chapter 6: Discovering What's Possible

1   This and a number of other conjectures can be found in Sarah Pruitt, "What Did Jesus Look Like?," History.com, February 20, 2019, https://www.history.com/news/what-did-jesus-look-like.

2   This appears alongside a broad set of other practices that support student success in Kuh and Schneider, *High-Impact Educational Practices*.

Chapter 7: Demystifying Discernment

1 Adam White, "Without Meaning: A Call for Radical Renewal in the Theology of Vocation," Church Anew, St. Andrew Lutheran Church, April 28, 2021, https://churchanew.org/blog/posts/adam-white-without-meaning-a-call-for-radical-renewal-in-the-theology-of-vocation.

2 Newberg and Waldman, *How God Changes Your Brain*.

Chapter 8: Developing Your Skills

1 If you want to find this inspiration as well, check out the Trinity United Church of Christ (Chicago) YouTube page: https://www.youtube.com/TRINITYCHGO.

2 Kuh and Schneider, *High-Impact Educational Practices*, 21.

Chapter 9: Deciding What's Next

1 Elie Wiesel, "Nobel Prize Speech," Elie Wiesel Foundation for Humanity, accessed January 29, 2022, https://eliewieselfoundation.org/elie-wiesel/nobelprizespeech/.

2 For an in-depth conversation on this, see Stephen Lewis, Matthew Wesley Williams, and Dori Grinenko Baker, *Another Way: Living and Leading Change on Purpose* (St. Louis, MO: Chalice Press, 2020).

3 Cynthia D. Moe-Lobeda, *Resisting Structural Evil: Love as Ecological-Economic Vocation* (Minneapolis: Fortress Press, 2013).

4 Parker J. Palmer, *A Hidden Wholeness: The Journey toward an Undivided Life* (Hoboken, NJ: Jossey-Bass, 2009).

5   Pema Chödrön, *This Moment Is the Perfect Teacher: 10 Buddhist Teachings on Cultivating Inner Strength and Compassion* (New York: Shambhala, 2008), audiobook.

6   "Navajo Chants," Natural History Museum of Utah, University of Utah, accessed May 27, 2021, https://nhmu.utah.edu/sites/default/files/attachments/Navajo%20Chants.pdf.

7   Eric Milner-White and G. W. Briggs, eds., *Daily Prayer* (London: Oxford University Press, 1941).

Recommended Resources

This collection includes resources referenced throughout the book as well as further reading to broaden your understanding of vocation and identity.

Christian Contributions to Vocation

Cahalan, Kathleen A., and Bonnie J. Miller-McLemore, eds. *Calling All Years Good: Christian Vocation throughout Life's Seasons.* Grand Rapids, MI: William B. Eerdmans, 2017.

    If you're curious about how vocation relates to specific eras of life, this text is for you. A variety of authors consider the implications of vocation in different stages of life, from childhood through adulthood. Writers provide conceptual frameworks and practices to adopt.

Moe-Lobeda, Cynthia D. *Resisting Structural Evil: Love as Ecological-Economic Vocation.* Minneapolis: Fortress Press, 2013.

    How does vocation relate to issues like the environmental crisis and the massive wealth disparities that characterize modern economies? Moe-Lobeda offers a compelling case that if human activity is responsible for the problems that threaten life today, so too humanity has the power to create change through the ways we perform our vocations.

Palmer, Parker J. *Let Your Life Speak: Listening for the Voice of Vocation.* San Francisco: Jossey-Bass, 1999.

    Palmer offers vocational wisdom from decades of personal experience as a Quaker, an academic, an activist, a spouse, a citizen, and more. While he follows Buechner by asserting a connection between gladness and vocation, examples provide some counterweight to that claim. An extended description of a clearness committee and an emphasis on the connectedness between individuals and the world we serve through our vocations are especially helpful.

Placher, William C., ed. *Callings: Twenty Centuries of Christian Wisdom on Vocation*. Grand Rapids, MI: William B. Eerdmans, 2005.

This resource details some of the ways Christians have approached vocation throughout history. Offering more historical and conceptual description than practical wisdom, these strands of thought may help you develop your own sense of vocation and how it operates in your life.

Wingren, Gustaf. *Luther on Vocation*. Eugene, OR: Wipf & Stock, 2004.

Sixteenth-century reformers didn't originate the idea of vocation, but they certainly did redefine it. Wingren provides a thorough introduction to the concept through the lens of Martin Luther's writings. Luther's work in the field is not only historically relevant but currently engaged by many scholars and practitioners of vocational exploration.

Traditions and Worldviews beyond Christianity

Cahalan, Kathleen A., and Douglas J. Schuurman, eds. *Calling in Today's World: Voices from Eight Faith Perspectives*. Grand Rapids, MI: William B. Eerdmans, 2016.

In this work, the authors write about vocation from a wide range of perspectives—secularist, Islamic, Hindu, Daoist, Jewish, and more. This is a great starting point for growing in your appreciation for other traditions' contributions to the conversation around vocation.

Dōgen, Eihei. *The True Dharma Eye: Zen Master Dōgen's Three Hundred Koans*. Translated by John Daido Loori and Kazuaki Tanahashi. Boston: Shambhala, 2009.

Koans are riddles used by Zen Buddhists in meditation and teaching to unearth deep truths. This collection from Zen master Dōgen includes many koans that relate to the concepts of action, work, identity, and being. Though it's unlikely Dōgen knew of vocation as a concept, the themes overlap in profound ways.

Easwaran, Eknath, trans. *The Bhagavad Gita*. Tomales, CA: Nilgiri Press, 2007.

This tale is a part of a larger epic collection of Hindu scriptures called the Mahabharata. An Indian prince named Arjuna converses with his guide, Krishna, an incarnation of Lord Vishnu, a deity. The Bhagavad Gita emphasizes, among other things, selflessness, service, and the cosmic connection of all life, which inspires reflection on the essence of meaning and a life worth living.

Grubin, David, dir. *The Buddha*. Arlington, VA: PBS, 2010. 112 minutes. https://www.amazon.com/Buddha-David-Grubin/dp/B004DAOITM.

Narrated by Richard Gere, this documentary explores the life of Siddhartha Gautama, the prince whose journey to enlightenment led him to become the Buddha. This foundational Buddhist story depicts the challenge of understanding the similarities and differences between identity and purpose, along with the liberation that is possible when proper differentiation arises.

Jain, Parveen. *An Introduction to Jain Philosophy*. San Jose, CA: Parveen and Neeraj Jain Endowment, 2019.

This book helpfully describes the interwoven concepts that make Jain Dharma a valuable way of life for many. With a long and successful business career in the United States, Parveen Jain introduces this Indian philosophy in terms accessible to Western readers.

Laozi. *Tao Te Ching*. Translated by Stephen Mitchell. New York: Harper Perennial, 1992.

The title roughly translated as "The Book of the Way," Laozi's foundational work addresses the nature of living through short sayings meant to inspire contemplation and conversation. This mode of teaching eschews the linear thought common to Western philosophy and religion and instead invites the reader to experience the energy of truth through the flow of reflection.

Ramadan, Tariq. *Introduction to Islam*. New York: Oxford University Press, 2017.

Though not specifically on vocation, this introductory text highlights many themes of purpose for Muslims. The necessity of generosity, the importance of ritual life, and the essential dignity of all humanity are only a few of the themes Ramadan describes. Especially helpful is the last section, which reflects on the contemporary challenges Muslims face in both identity and vocation.

Sefaria. "A Living Library of Jewish Texts Online." Living Library of Torah. Accessed December 20, 2021. https://www.sefaria.org/.

This site collects the reflections of Jewish authorities throughout the ages. Organized both by topic (such as holidays, social issues, and art) and by text (from the Hebrew Bible to legal applications and mystical interpretations), Sefaria provides an array of resources for both lifelong Jews and those not previously exposed to the tradition. While all are worth your attention, sections such as "Talmud," "Midrash," "Kabbalah," and "Jewish Thought" resonate more frequently with vocation.

Stedman, Chris. *Faitheist: How an Atheist Found Common Ground with the Religious*. Boston: Beacon Press, 2013.

This story reveals the vital role that atheism and other secular and nonreligious approaches to meaning can play in conversations about vocation. In fact, Stedman's ultimate argument is that atheists have a call to engage in dialogues about religious diversity because they enrich the conversation and are, in turn, enriched by it through the embodiment of that vocation.

Examples of Vocational Journeys

Cohen, Julie, and Betsy West, dirs. *My Name Is Pauli Murray*. Culver City, CA: Amazon Studios, 2021. 133 minutes. https://www.amazon.com/My-Name-Pauli-Murray/dp/B09DMPMWCP.

This documentary on Pauli Murray's life introduces her/his story in a compelling format, more fully enfleshing the vocational transitions Pauli made throughout life. If you prefer a written resource, check out Rosalind Rosenberg's *Jane Crow: The Life of Pauli Murray* (New York: Oxford University Press, 2020). Both lift up Pauli's legacy as one with great relevance for today's vocational explorers.

Curtice, Kaitlin B. *Native: Identity, Belonging, and Rediscovering God*. Grand Rapids, MI: Brazos Press, 2020.

Kaitlin Curtice challenges and inspires readers as she engages questions of identity and vocation, especially as they relate to her Christian faith and her citizenship in the Citizen Potawatomi Nation. This is an especially helpful read for those who feel an internal conflict between different identities or between identities and vocations.

Duncan, Lenny. *United States of Grace: A Memoir of Home-lessness, Addiction, Incarceration, and Hope.* Minneapolis: Broadleaf Books, 2021.

However obvious the intersections of identity and vocation are in the book's title, it is in Duncan's story that they move from the head to penetrate the heart. For those who want to consider the relationship of race and sexual orientation to other aspects of identity as well as notions of vocation, this book is a touchstone.

Fujimura, Makoto. *Refractions: A Journey of Faith, Art, and Culture.* Colorado Springs: NavPress, 2009.

Not only does this book more fully engage the metaphor of a prism; it also reveals how traumatic events can force us to reevaluate our sense of self and purpose. Fujimura, living in New York on 9/11, is forever changed by the events of that day, something that he processes through the vocations of painting and writing.

Kegler, Emmy. *One Coin Found: How God's Love Stretches to the Margins.* Minneapolis: Fortress Press, 2019.

This book details Kegler's story of call as well as how that call was challenged by both internal and external forces. As a queer Christian, she faced both external prejudices and internal questions as the result of those challenges, especially as they relate to biblical interpretation. Her story emphasizes that even when we feel isolated, we're not outside the realm of divine love or beyond the reach of sacred calling.

Practical Resources

Gazelle, Gail. *Everyday Resilience: A Practical Guide to Build Inner Strength and Weather Life's Challenges.* Emeryville, CA: Rockridge Press, 2020.

Though not specifically addressing issues of vocation or identity, resilience is a necessary trait for those who encounter obstacles on their vocational journeys. Odds are, everyone does. The actions Gazelle recommends are proven effective through scientific research and presented in an easily digestible, practical manner.

Kuh, George D., and Carol Geary Schneider. *High-Impact Educational Practices: What They Are, Who Has Access to Them, and Why They Matter.* Washington, DC: Association of American Colleges and Universities, 2008.

At first glance, this book may not seem relevant to your life, especially if you're not a college student or university employee. Yet the longitudinal research that undergirds the book shows that the practices it recommends helped students persist in education and achieve their goals with higher rates of success than their peers who did not utilize similar practices. These practices could prove equally effective for you.

Kunkel, Mary Clare, ed. *NOW+NEXT.* Capital University Center for Faith and Learning. Accessed December 21, 2021. https://anchor.fm/capital-university-cfl.

The *NOW+NEXT* podcast explores vocation through discussions about "your meaningful now and meaningful next." Through conversations with authors, researchers, practitioners, and everyday people, each season discusses themes such as embodiment and art and includes prolonged discussions on 4D Formation.

Lewis, Stephen, Matthew Wesley Williams, and Dori Grinenko Baker. *Another Way: Living and Leading Change on Purpose*. St. Louis, MO: Chalice Press, 2020.

Designed specifically for communal discernment processing, *Another Way* provides an intentional approach to change that emphasizes broad buy-in and participation. The practices focus on creating space to ask questions that inspire both theological reflection and specific action. With multiple authors of color, this book also centers perspectives that are not often amplified in vocational exploration.

Moser, Drew, and Chuck DeGroat. *The Enneagram of Discernment: The Way of Vocation, Wisdom, and Practice*. Beaver Falls, PA: Falls City Press, 2020.

The Enneagram is a personality-typing resource that has gained popularity in recent years. This resource applies the Enneagram specifically to vocational exploration. The authors give special focus to how each of the nine types can challenge and benefit your sense of purpose as well as how they may relate to your identities.

Network for Vocation in Undergraduate Education (NetVUE). "About NetVUE." Council of Independent Colleges. Accessed December 21, 2021. https://www.cic.edu/programs/NetVUE.

NetVUE is an organization of colleges and universities that prioritize vocational exploration in their classes and extracurricular experiences. While most colleges in the network have historical affiliations with Christianity, the faculty, staff, and administrators involved come from diverse religious traditions and worldviews. The page offers a variety of resources, including a map of the member institutions, a collection of vocation publications, and a blog by practitioners that explores the most recent themes in vocational studies.

Newberg, Andrew B., and Mark Robert Waldman. *How God Changes Your Brain: Breakthrough Findings from a Leading Neuroscientist*. New York: Ballantine Books, 2010.

This blend of research findings and practical applications draws on the realms of neuroscience and psychology. The findings show that through simple, ritual practices, you can increase compassion, decrease anxiety, and foster other beneficial traits. Not only can this make your journey more manageable; it can also help you more strongly distinguish between your identity and your behaviors.

Thibodeaux, Mark E. *Reimagining the Ignatian Examen: Fresh Ways to Pray from Your Day*. Chicago: Loyola Press, 2015.

The *examen* is a prayer of examination developed by Saint Ignatius of Loyola. Thibodeaux introduces the classic practice and then offers over thirty adaptations for modern life. The ritual provides a daily contemplative experience that invites deepened gratitude and increased clarity on not only your day but how you relate to your environment, your actions, your faith, and your purpose.